Reflections on
American Indian History

Reflections on American Indian History

Honoring the Past, Building a Future

Edited by Albert L. Hurtado

Introduction by Wilma Mankiller

University of Oklahoma Press : Norman

Also by Albert L. Hurtado

Indian Survival on the California Frontier (New Haven, 1988)
(ed., with Peter Iverson) *Major Problems in American Indian
    History: Documents and Essays* (Lexington, 1994; Boston,
    2001)
Intimate Frontiers: Sex, Gender, and Culture in Old California
    (Albuquerque, 1999)
John Sutter: A Life on the North American Frontier (Norman,
    2006)

Library of Congress Cataloging-in-Publication Data

Reflections on American Indian history : honoring the past, building a
future / edited by Albert L. Hurtado ; introduction by Wilma Mankiller.
        p.   cm.
    Includes index.
    "Originated from the Wilma Mankiller Symposium on American
History, sponsored by the University of Oklahoma . . . held at the University Memorial Union on April 12 and 13, 2005"—Pref.
    ISBN 978-0-8061-3896-1 (hardcover : alk. paper)
    1. Indians of North America—History. 2. Indians of North America—
Government relations. 3. United States—Ethnic relations. 4. United
States—History. I. Hurtado, Albert L., 1946– II. Wilma Mankiller Sym-
posium on American History (2005 : University of Oklahoma)
    E76.W55 2005
    973.04'97—dc22
                                                        2007025269

The paper in this book meets the guidelines for permanence and dura-
bility of the Committee on Production Guidelines for Book Longevity of
the Council on Library Resources. ∞

1 2 3 4 5 6 7 8 9 10

Contents

Preface

Albert L. Hurtado

This volume of essays originated from the Wilma Mankiller Symposium on American History, sponsored by the University of Oklahoma. The symposium, held at the University Memorial Union on April 12 and 13, 2005, grew out of an occasional series of public lectures funded by the University of Oklahoma and the Travis and Merrick chairs in American history.[1] The success of these annual events encouraged the history department to organize a lecture symposium in honor of an important Oklahoman that would bring together a small group of leading scholars to speak on an important aspect of western American history. Their essays would comprise a short interpretive volume to be published by the University of Oklahoma Press.

We did not have to look far to find an appropriate namesake for the symposium. Wilma Mankiller graciously consented to lend her name to the endeavor. She is one of the most significant westerners of her generation. A noted activist in the Native American rights movement, feminist, and former principal chief of the Cherokee Nation, Chief Mankiller led the way in the revitalization of tribal governments that marked the last quarter of the twentieth century. Her unflagging efforts on behalf of the Cherokees and other Native Americans have earned her the respect of all Americans. President Clinton awarded her the Medal of Freedom, the highest civilian decoration given by the U.S. government.[2]

The Mankiller Symposium quickly attracted generous donors who wished to honor her and to support scholarship. Oklahoma donors include Clifford and Leslie Hudson, Jim and Christy Everest, Paul G. Heafy, and Gene and Jeannine Rainbolt. Clifford Hudson deserves special mention for leading the drive for private funding and for suggesting that the symposium be named for Chief Mankiller. The redoubtable chair of the history department, Robert Griswold, devoted his time, energy, and talents to organizing and funding this event. The Ford Foundation provided a significant grant for the Mankiller Symposium. The offices of David Boren, president of the University of Oklahoma, and Paul Bell, dean of the College of Arts and Sciences, provided additional funding. The University of Oklahoma Press has enthusiastically supported this project. The history department wishes to thank all of these individuals and institutions for making this volume possible. The department owes a special debt to Dr. George Milne, who was a doctoral student at the time of the symposium, for taking charge of the myriad details associated with staging the event.

It did not take long to decide what the general theme should be for the symposium. Native American history in the twentieth century was not only an obvious subject but an important one to the people of Oklahoma, to thoughtful Americans everywhere, and to Chief Mankiller. The contributors were asked to think broadly about Native American history in the twentieth century but were otherwise left free to choose topics and approaches. Nevertheless, the lectures and the revised essays presented here are a remarkably coherent body of thought about themes that are central to Native American studies today. Each of the authors has given attention to the ways in which history continues to influence contemporary Native American life. Yet, this is not a collection of screeds complaining about past victimization and current exploitation. Rather, the authors see a hopeful future that is rooted in Native historical consciousness, resilience, tradition, and adaptability.

A revised version of Chief Mankiller's banquet address, presented here as the volume's introduction, sets the tone for the essays that follow. While acknowledging the losses that tribes suffered in the past, Chief Mankiller emphasizes the continuing efforts of Native people to preserve and defend their cultures, languages, and tribal sovereignty. The tone of her address is optimistic and forward looking. Contemporary Indian culture is firmly rooted in the past, she says, and Indian people look to the future with faith, pride, and hope.

Colin Calloway provides a broad, thoughtful essay that outlines the major themes of Indian history that continue to resonate today—colonialism, land and treaty rights, sovereignty, wealth and poverty, and culture and identity. Calloway is known primarily as a colonialist. His comprehensive understanding of the early period of Native American history equips him to describe the connections between the deep past and the living present. The past is not something that Indians seek to escape but a bridge to the future. Calloway's grandfather's axe—an imaginary tool that is continuously refashioned in order to meet new exigencies—symbolizes the importance of cultural continuity and flexibility that mark Indian history.

R. David Edmunds's essay illustrates how Native people adapted to changing circumstances while selectively adopting cultural changes and modes of living from the new choices that emerged in the twentieth century. Drawing on his profound knowledge of Indian history, Edmunds sketches a hypothetical portrait of so-called traditional and progressive Indians, showing that even these problematic and stereotypical images have changed over time. As with Calloway, adaptability is a key theme in Edmunds's essay.

Laurence M. Hauptman shows how the Oneida community interprets its past and draws strength from its history. Here we see how the past impinges on the Oneidas' sense of identity. Oneida history is told and retold because it tells them who they are while explaining their relationship with state and federal governments. As Hauptman shows, Oneida history is not always strictly correct or verifiable in the ways that academic historians usually think of their work. But it is full of meaning and truth for the Oneidas because it validates their conception of personal and tribal identity as well as historic relations with the U.S. government.

Peter Iverson elaborates on the themes of Indian survival and persistence while explaining that historians have not always sympathetically or accurately written about Indian history. Iverson urges historians to give more attention to Indian successes in the last few decades instead of the losses of the nineteenth century. Surely, he argues, recent Indian history is more optimistic (and perhaps more predictive of future developments) than rehashes of the Indian wars and reservation confinement. Problems remain, but so does hope that Indians will find solutions that are efficacious and uniquely their own.

Brenda Child's concluding essay circles back to Chief Mankiller. The perseverance of the jingle dress tradition illustrates how time-honored practices continue to invigorate Ojibwe life alongside modern medicine. Child embeds in her essay about cultural persistence the story of anthropologist Frances Densmore, who did field work among the Ojibwes in the first half of the twentieth century. Among the Ojibwes, Densmore learned, the world of women and women's work was instrumental in carrying traditions forward.

Taken together, these essays show how these leading scholars think about Native American history today. Their work delineates a hopeful vision for the field of Native American studies and the future of Native American people. This volume is offered in the hope that it will in some measure influence future Native American scholarship.

Notes

1. Travis-Merrick lecturers have included Elliot West, Patricia Limerick, David Weber, William Taylor, and Vicki Ruiz.

2. Wilma Mankiller and Michael Wallis, *Mankiller: A Chief and Her People* (New York: St. Martin's Press, 1993), 274 and passim.

Introduction

Wilma Mankiller

There are more than 550 diverse tribal governments in the United States, each with its own unique history, culture, and language. The forms of government range from the elective systems of the Cherokees and Navajos to the Onondagas, where the women select male chiefs to lead their nation. The land base and population of tribes range from the Navajos, with millions of acres of land and more than 250,000 enrolled members, to some California tribal governments with fewer than fifty acres of land and fewer than 100 members.

It is apparent from public discourse that many people still do not realize that tribal governments predate the U.S. government and that there is a long history of government-to-government relations between the United States and indigenous nations. And even fewer know that well before the United States came into being, tribal people living on this land now called America developed a kind of United Nations among the warring Haudenosaunee (or Iroquois). The tribes formed the Iroquois Confederacy, an organization that remains in existence today, for the purpose of peace, trade, and friendship.

When the United States was in its infancy, the federal government recognized tribal sovereignty in formal treaties with indigenous nations. Between 1779, when the Delawares signed the first peace treaty with the United States, and 1871, when the treaty-making era ended, the United States executed and the Senate ratified 370 formal treaties with Native nations. Though the U.S. Supreme Court recognizes treaties as valid legal instruments and statements of federal policy, they have rarely been fully honored by the U.S. Congress and executive branch.

According to the First Nations Development Institute, by the early twentieth century the United States had taken possession of more than two billion acres of Indian land by treaty or official government confiscation. Entire tribal nations were forcibly removed from their confiscated homelands, including my own people, the Cherokees, who were marched like cattle across several states from their southeastern homelands to Indian Territory, now Oklahoma. The story of the Cherokee removal is similar to the story of many other tribal groups, not in detail, but in net effect.

With this historical backdrop and context, tribal people and their governments today are waging a fierce battle to protect their remaining land base and sovereign rights. This fight for treaty rights and sovereignty is made immeasurably more difficult by the fact that so few Americans understand our history or contemporary lives. Besides the fight for sovereignty, tribal people are also fighting to retain the tribal lifeways, culture, and languages that have sustained them since time immemorial, as the scholars in this volume demonstrate.

What do I mean by indigenous culture and lifeways, and why is it important that we maintain them? Some people describe cultural attributes as language, medicine, song, ceremony, land, and community, and some simply define culture as lifeways. In Native communities, the response to the question of what constitutes culture will vary from community to community and individual to individual, although there is probably general agreement that living according to a certain set of values is one of the most important attributes of culture. Traditional indigenous values such as reciprocity and a sense of interdependence can be maintained whether one lives in an urban area or on tribal homelands.

Most non-Native Americans know little about the governments of indigenous people and even less about the values and lifeways of indigenous people. This lack of accurate information has produced a number of stereotypes, including that of the mystical child of nature—spiritual but incapable of higher thought—or the bloodthirsty savage who murdered and scalped innocent settlers. Whether indigenous people are romanticized or vilified, they are rarely viewed as whole human beings. After all these years of interaction with those around us, indigenous people seem to have no identity with outsiders except that which has been created by stereotypes.

A significant number of people believe tribal people still live and dress as they did three hundred years ago. During my tenure as principal chief of the Cherokee Nation, the summer would bring tourists who sometimes expressed disappointment when they saw no tipis or tribal people dressed in buckskin on Main Street. When these crestfallen tourists asked, "Where are all the Indians?" I sometimes placed my tongue in cheek and responded, quite truthfully, "They are probably at Wal-Mart."

Though many non-Native Americans have learned little about us, over time we have had to learn much about them. We watch their films, read their literature, worship in their churches, and attend their schools. Every third-grade student in the United States is presented with the concept of Europeans discovering America as a "new world." Only the most enlightened teachers will explain that this world certainly was not new to the millions of indigenous people who already lived here when Columbus accidentally stumbled onto our shores.

People in the United States fail to recognize how much they have been influenced by indigenous people. It is simply amazing that even after hundreds of years of living in our former villages, most Americans do not know much about the original people of this land. Anthropologist Jack Weatherford, who traces the birth of modern pharmacology to indigenous people, argues that America has yet to be discovered. Weatherford documents many other important but little-known Native American contributions to knowledge.

It has always been of interest to me that in the many dozens of national and international discussions and debates about the need to preserve the Arctic National Wildlife Refuge or the South American Amazon, indigenous people are rarely even mentioned or considered, though the people have lived with these lands for thousands of years and have a tremendous amount of knowledge to share. For many tradition-oriented Native people, environmentalism is not an intellectual exercise or work they are engaged in; rather, it is their life.

The knowledge and culture of indigenous people hold many potential gifts for the world. One of the most important challenges of our time is to figure out the best way to capture and maintain traditional knowledge systems. Whenever a traditional elder passes on, they take with them thousands of years of unique knowledge that had been passed down from generation to generation. This tribal knowledge gives Native people a sense of identity, of belonging, of knowing their place in the world. In the larger society around us, there is little recognition of the importance of maintaining traditional indigenous knowledge. In some cases, our people remain objects of curiosity instead of people with important knowledge to share.

Over the centuries there have been a number of concerted efforts to assimilate Native people into the larger Euro-American culture. But I am not sure exactly what attributes of American culture assimilationists want us to adopt. Most Americans who advocate Native American assimilation are hard-pressed to define American culture. If one looks at television reality shows and popular culture, it would appear that a high premium is placed on individual wealth and personal appearance, that greed is the norm, and that kindness is often perceived as a weakness. Are these the new values that Native people should now espouse?

To be sure, tribal cultures have been dramatically affected by the world around them, but in every community, no matter how troubled, one can find a core group of people who are responsible for maintaining a strong sense of community and working to maintain tribal values, traditions, and lifeways. It is remarkable that indigenous people continue to value traditional knowledge after the staggering amount of adversity they have faced. Certainly our attachment to tribal values has contributed to our survival and well-being. If we are still standing after everything that has happened to us historically, surely we can be optimistic about the future.

Native people have suffered great losses. Some indigenous languages have vanished, while others are endangered. Some of the old ceremonies have been lost over time, and our communities are no longer as intact as they once were. But ancient traditional knowledge and values, such as reciprocity and a sense of interdependence with one another and with the land, continue to inform the contemporary lives of indigenous people. They are held together in relationships and interdependence by a common understanding of history, culture, and, most important, values.

I am often asked why I remain optimistic about the future of indigenous communities and governments given the litany of social and economic problems we face. As always, we need only to look back to the past to see our future. We have endured war, removal, loss of land, resources, and rights, and wholesale attempts to assimilate us, and yet we continue to have strong, viable indigenous communities. If we have managed to hold onto a robust sense of who we are despite the staggering amount of adversity we have faced, how can we not be optimistic? After every major upheaval, we have almost had to reinvent ourselves as a people, but we have never given up our sense of community, of clan, of family, of nation. Despite everything, we rejoice in the knowledge that ceremonies given to us by the Creator continue, that the original languages are still spoken, and that our governments remain strong. We acknowledge the hardships of the past without dwelling on them. Instead, we look to the future with the same faith that kept us together thus far. The Mohawks speak for all when they say, "It is hard to see the future with tears in your eyes." With no tears in our eyes, we accept our responsibility to make sure those who come after us will always know what it means to be descendants of the original people of this land called America.

Reflections on
American Indian History

Chapter 1

My Grandfather's Axe

Living with a Native American Past

Colin G. Calloway

All of us who do Indian history will have been chastised at one time or another by Indian people for focusing on the past, contributing to the stereotype that Indians lived then, not now, and diverting attention from contemporary presence, problems, and achievements. They are right, of course, to a point. But as Indian people have demanded attention and demonstrated beyond any question that they are still here, I sometimes have detected quite the opposite problem: people pay little or no attention to the historical roots of what was happening. In that sense, Indians in modern America suffer from too little history, not too much.

To say we need to understand the past to make sense of the present is not to say anything new.[1] It is said that if you never know what happened before you were born you will always remain a child. That is also true of nations, especially one whose citizens ask, "Why did all the Anasazis live in national parks?" and whose national mythology portrays historical figures like George Washington and Lewis and Clark with their eyes fixed on distant horizons, on the future.[2] If you walk along with your eyes fixed on the horizon, you will surely step in something along the way. If you keep your eyes fixed on the horizon, you may not even know you stepped in it, and you'll probably step in it again and again. If you walk along looking backward, you are just as likely to step in stuff, but at least you'll know it happened. I've heard Indian colleagues say there's little point trying to look ahead to the future: you can't foresee what is going to happen; it will sneak up on you. You can only see what happened in the past.[3]

But being British and chairing a Native American studies program, as I have done for the past ten years, I often find myself having conversations with people who do not see the long arm of history. They find it intriguing that a Brit is chairing a Native American studies program. Sometimes they say, "That's great!" but usually with a chuckle. They also, often, feel compelled to tell me a thing or two about how things really are with Indians in this country. They may acknowledge that Indians got a raw deal, but for the most part they adopt a "get over it" attitude. In their minds, Indian cultural, political, and economic aspirations that came to the fore in the late twentieth century came out of nowhere and should be treated as modern fads.[4] As a historian, I take the opposite view. Rather than review the well-known negative legacies of U.S. Indian policy, I will offer some reflections on the issues that seem to bother the people who bother me— colonialism, land and treaty rights, sovereignty, wealth and poverty, and culture and identity—unresolved issues that are rooted in the past.

Colonialism

Critics of present-day Native American claims, successes, failures, and distinct political status often do not take account of colonialism, and sometimes refuse to consider it. In this country, the word "colonial" conjures up images of Williamsburg and Benjamin Franklin, of three-cornered hats and knee breeches, a quaint prelude to the real business of American history ushered in by George Washington and his fellow patriots. To acknowledge that colonialism has continued to shape Native American lives and choices long after the colonial era ended for white Americans requires accepting that colonial ways of thinking might persist in modern attitudes about race and gender, family and community, culture and identity, and history. Colonialism is not just about holding distant lands and peoples in subjugation; it is about establishing and perpetuating systems of power. As Edward W. Said wrote about imperialism, it "lingers where it has always been, in a kind of general cultural sphere as well as in specific political, ideological, economic, and social practices."[5] And, as Anishinabe legal scholar John Borrows says, "colonial pathologies . . . continue to resonate within our communities."[6] Colonialism exerts power over narratives of the past as well as over lives and resources. History is contested ground: Who owns it? Who records it and how? Who writes it and why? Whose story gets to be told? Native people who feel that enduring colonial structures and attitudes stifle their voices and distort their historical experiences insist that Indian people should write, or not write, their own histories and that Indian communities should control the use of knowledge from those communities. Some non-Natives argue that Indian control over Indian history will undermine academic standards and misrepresent their version of U.S. history.[7]

The United States cannot simply wish away its colonial past—if that were possible I suspect Native people would have wished it away long since—but it seems equally unable to acknowledge a colonial present. Public perceptions of colonialism are more likely informed by Mel Gibson than by Edward Said. In a nation that claims a monopoly on freedom, who will hear complaints from the unfree as anything but un-American? In the eighteenth century and nineteenth century to be a Native person was to be in a colonial relationship. Those of us who are not on the wrong end of it might not easily see such a relationship today, but that does not mean that colonialism is not still alive and kicking.

Land and Treaty Rights

In its treaties with Indian nations, the United States often acknowledged the boundaries of reserved tribal lands, recognized the right to continue hunting and fishing on ceded lands, and recognized tribal sovereignty. But treaties were also instruments of dispossession that, together with the often unspoken motivations of federal policy makers, embody the essence of American colonialism. Converting Indian homelands into American real estate is a time-honored, if generally dishonorable, practice. The nation was built on it. Thomas Jefferson and his contemporaries framed U.S. Indian policy around it: Promise just and humanitarian dealings with Indian people but commit the nation to expansion into Indian lands. Invoke the limited power of government to do nothing when American citizens encroach on Indian lands but apply federal power to suppress Indians' resistance. Exact Indian lands as the price of peace, and allow the process to begin again. Encourage Indians to run up debts at trading posts then make them sell tribal lands to settle the bill. Ignore the fact that Indian women in the eastern woodlands had been farming for hundreds of years and turn the men into farmers—farmers need less land than hunters. Invite Indian people to assimilate into American society but ensure their exclusion and removal.[8] Tribal leaders in the eighteenth and nineteenth centuries signed treaties transferring millions of acres of land; allotment took millions more. Tribal leaders in the twentieth century signed agreements permitting the extraction of millions of tons of energy resources. Ojibwa timber, Osage oil, Navajo coal and uranium, water, all were up for grabs.[9] Tribal lands and resources passed into American hands, and the payments slipped through Indian fingers, siphoned off by poverty, deceit, and greed.

Indians resisted the process, of course. In the eighteenth and nineteenth centuries, multitribal coalitions confronted the British empire and American invasion and defended an alternative vision of America. In the later twentieth century, the Council of Energy Resource Tribes (CERT), moratoria on coal mining, lobbying in Congress, alliances with environmental groups, management, and mediation put an end to the days when taking Indian resources could be taken for granted.[10] And Indians have defended and asserted their treaty rights in the courts.

Successful assertions of Indian rights in court often produce a backlash. Some Indian communities have tried to
recover land they lost through lawsuit or purchase. Critics
have called it "buying up" land and depict it as both threatening and somehow unnatural. What worries them, of course,
is not the buying and selling of land but the direction of the
transaction. "You can't turn back the clock," they say; "they
sold the land, didn't they?" The fact that tribal leaders ceded
huge chunks of America with inadequate compensation, with
inappropriate representation at the treaty councils and in
Washington, with incomplete understanding of the terms, or
with their judgment clouded by fear or alcohol is dismissed as
"ancient history." So what if treaties were broken? There is
nothing we can do about it now without initiating another
round of injustices by penalizing current landowners for the
actions of their ancestors or, worse still, of someone else's
ancestors.[11] Others complain that recognizing tribes' land,
fishing, or water rights and their sovereign rights within the
reservation is unfair, even discriminatory, since it gives Indians
"special rights" not enjoyed by the non-Indian population.

As legal scholar Charles Wilkinson points out, "Indian
rights are indeed 'special' in that they are uniquely complex
and history-based, emerging from the distant past rather than
arising from well-known modern circumstances."[12] Treaties
were, and remain, the law of the land and, as Justice Hugo
Black said when the Army Corps of Engineers ignored historic treaty commitments and flooded ten thousand acres of
Seneca lands to create the Kinzua Dam in 1964, "Great
nations like great men should keep their word."[13] In Canada
the 1763 Proclamation, established by Crown authority but
negotiated in Indian country through treaty council, continues

to have vital relevance today as the basis for dealings between the government and the First Nations. The proclamation's provision that Indian peoples held rights to unceded lands, and that those rights could be alienated only by surrendering them to the Crown or its agents, remains a fundamental document of Native rights and sovereignty.[14]

In the United States, the Northwest Ordinance of 1787 declared, "The utmost good faith shall always be observed towards the Indians, their lands and property shall never be taken from them without their consent; and in their property, rights and liberty, they never shall be invaded or disturbed, *unless in just and lawful wars authorised by Congress*" (emphasis added).[15] The Indian Trade and Intercourse Act of 1790 stipulated that no purchases of Indian land were valid without congressional approval. It provided the Penobscots and Passamaquoddies with a solid claim for the return of those lands that the states of Massachusetts and Maine purchased without congressional approval—about two-thirds of the state of Maine. In 1980 the U.S. government awarded the Penobscots and Passamaquoddies $81.5 million in compensation, a shock to many non-Indians in the area, few of whom knew much about Indian law or Indian history or even that there were still Indians in Maine.[16] The same year the U.S. Supreme Court awarded the Sioux $122 million, recognizing the validity of the long Sioux fight against the theft of the Black Hills in violation of the 1868 Treaty of Fort Laramie, although it did not, of course, return the Hills.[17] Mid-nineteenth-century treaties provided the legal basis for Great Lakes and Pacific Northwest tribes to reassert their fishing rights in the second half of the twentieth century.[18]

Treaties are not dead, dusty, and irrelevant documents; they are alive, and they have power.[19] We invoke other eighteenth-century documents—the Declaration of Independence and the Constitution, for instance—as guides from the past to proper action and moral values in our modern world; indeed, those documents hold a certain sacred power. Why not accord Indian treaties and the Supreme Court cases that laid the foundations of federal Indian law with the same reverence? They too were essential documents in building the nation. Laudatory biographies crowding the shelves at Borders and Barnes and Noble make the founding fathers look like demigods, but Indian treaties show that they dealt in half-truths as well as self-evident truths. Contrary to what some would have us believe, to acknowledge their hypocrisy and human failing is not heresy, just history. Thomas Jefferson wrote that "a bigoted veneration for the supposed superlative wisdom of their fathers" chained people to barbarism.[20] He was referring to Indians, but similar veneration for Jefferson and his peers should not blind us to their actions or excuse us from the commitments they made when their actions were less than exemplary.

Sovereignty

Sovereignty lies at the heart of tribal survival, but tribal sovereignty is often treated as an oxymoron: Native peoples were never sufficiently sophisticated politically to understand what sovereignty was, or if they did have it, they quickly lost it. Native assertions of sovereignty and aspirations to nations-within-a-nation status are twentieth-century inventions, something that sprang up when Indians started "getting political."

But Indians have always been political. Watch a PBS documentary and you hear Indians talking, with flute music in the background, about what it means to be a spiritual person and to live in harmony with the earth. Read eighteenth-century documents and you hear Indian people asserting their sovereignty and their determination to preserve their land and independence. European nations recognized Indian sovereignty, and particularly their right to the soil, if only as a means of legitimizing their acquisition of Indian land in the face of competition from other nations. Indian speakers frequently reminded them of that sovereignty.

In 1727, for example, the English made a treaty with the Indians of Maine—the "Eastern Indians"—at Casco Bay. The English text describes it as a treaty of "submission" in which the Indians admit responsibility for the past war, open their lands to Englishmen, and agree to be ruled by English law. A Penobscot sachem, Loron Sauguaarum, remembered things very differently and gave a point-by-point refutation of the written treaty, which, he said, appeared "to contain things which are not." He rejected any notion of submission. Yes, he had recognized that the king of England was sovereign over the king's lands but clarified, "Do not hence infer that I acknowledge thy King as my King, and King of my lands. Here lies my distinction—my Indian distinction. God hath willed that I have no King, and that I be master of my lands in common."[21]

As Britain and France competed for hegemony in North America, Indians stressed that their independence and sovereignty were nonnegotiable. An Abenaki chief named Atiwanto told the English in no uncertain terms that the Abenakis would fight them because they refused to give up "a single inch" more land, not because they were allied to the French: "We are entirely free," Atiwanto declared.[22] Indians were "not governed by the French," announced a Huron, "but were free all over the world."[23] Captain Pierre Pouchot, the French commander at Fort Niagara, said Indians refused "to recognize any foreigner as their master, just as they have none among themselves."[24] Irish trader-agent George Croghan reckoned Indians had "the highest notions of Liberty of any people on Earth" and "will never Consider Consequences when they think their Liberty likely to be invaded, tho' it may End in their Ruin." All Indians, he said, "from their high Notions of Liberty hate power."[25] "The Iroquois laugh when you talk to them of obedience to kings," wrote trader John Long. "They cannot reconcile submission with the dignity of man. Each individual is a sovereign in his own mind, and as he conceives he derives his freedom from the Great Spirit alone, he cannot be induced to acknowledge any other power."[26]

Traveling in the Ohio country before the American Revolution, Reverend David Jones observed that Shawnees were "strangers to civil power and authority." They believed, he said, that God made them free and that "one man has no natural right to rule over another." On this point, noted Jones (several years before Thomas Jefferson inscribed his self-evident truths in the Declaration of Independence), "they agree with our greatest politicians, who affirm that a ruler's authority extends no further than the pleasure of the people, and when any exceeds that power given, it may be justly asked, by what authority doest thou these things, and who gave thee that authority?"[27] The U.S. Constitution recognized Indian sovereignty, and Jefferson spoke of the Indians' "full, undivided and independent sovereignty, as long as they choose to keep it."[28]

Indians used colonial courts to seek legal protection and redress of grievances; they used the U.S. Supreme Court to defend their sovereignty. The Cherokee cases are well known as establishing the baseline for federal Indian law. In considering *Cherokee Nation v. Georgia* in 1831 Chief Justice John Marshall described Indian tribes as "domestic dependent nations." In *Worcester v. Georgia* the next year, the court found that a state had no authority to execute its laws within an Indian nation protected under the treaty clause of the U.S. Constitution. A couple of decades later, in a case not specifically about Indians, another chief justice described them as "a free and independent people, associated together in nations or tribes, and governed by their own laws. . . . These Indian Governments were regarded and treated as foreign Governments, as much so as if an ocean had separated the red man from the white; and their freedom has constantly been acknowledged, from the time of the first emigration to the English colonies to the present day, by the different Governments which succeeded each other." The chief justice was Roger Taney, and the case was *Dred Scott v. Sandford.* Despite "the course of events" that had rendered them subject to the white race, Taney seemed clear about the sovereign status of Indian nations.[29]

So did the Supreme Court in 1883. It freed the Brule chief Crow Dog, who had been arrested for the murder of Spotted Tail. There was no question Crow Dog did it—Crow Dog's family gave Spotted Tail's family six hundred dollars, eight ponies, and a blanket to redress the killing and restore tribal harmony in accordance with Brule law. The question was whether he could be tried in Dakota territorial court and hanged for the crime. The answer was no. On appeal, the U.S. Supreme Court held that American Indians, as sovereign nations, were subject to their own laws: a crime committed by one Indian against another in Indian Country was subject to Indian law. Crow Dog walked free. That was the law of the United States in 1883.[30]

Congress responded to the Crow Dog decision by passing the Major Crimes Act in 1885. The next year the Supreme Court reaffirmed the constitutionality of this federal intrusion into tribal jurisdiction in *United States v. Kagama*.[31] Then in 1903 the Supreme Court asserted the plenary power of Congress over Indian lands.[32] Since then, key pieces of the bundle of rights—reserved rights—that constitute tribal sovereignty have come under assault. For example, *Oliphant v. Suquamish* in 1978 robbed tribes of criminal jurisdiction over non-Indians on their reservations; *Nevada v. Hicks* in 2001 deprived tribes of civil jurisdiction over the conduct of state officials operating on their reservations. Many casino tribes have signed compacts with states, as required by the Indian Gaming Regulatory Act, and in doing so, critics argue, have compromised their sovereignty. Indian people protect and preserve their sovereign rights by daily struggle, reaffirm them by countless small acts, and reassert them repeatedly lest they fall victim to the use-it-or-lose-it philosophy.

Often they do so in the face of considerable hostility and from positions of considerable weakness. In Vermont, the Abenakis have repeatedly challenged the state on issues of reburial and repatriation, recognition, and sovereignty. The Abenakis have never had U.S. recognition as an Indian tribe, although they first applied for it more than twenty years ago. They received state recognition briefly, when Governor Thomas Salmon conferred it in November 1976, and then Governor Richard Snelling rescinded it in 1977. Atiwanto had told the English 224 years before, "The lands we possess have been given us by the Master of Life." Governor Snelling told *Yankee* magazine, "When they told me the land was given to them by God, I told them what I couldn't find was where God registered the deed."[33]

Abenakis staged acts of civil disobedience challenging the state of Vermont's authority. They held fish-ins on the Missisquoi River, got arrested for fishing out of season and without licenses, and argued that the state had no jurisdiction over them as members of a sovereign nation. The Missisquoi Abenaki Nation of Vermont also provided its members with Abenaki license plates. After the 1987 "fish-in" the state finally went to trial. The state court judge dismissed the charges: ruling that the state had failed to prove that the Abenakis had ceded their lands, he recognized the Abenakis' right to hunt year-round in three counties. In 1992 the Vermont Supreme Court overturned the decision. According to the superior court, aboriginal rights could be extinguished "by the increasing weight of history."[34] The state dismissed most of the charges and passed a bill granting the Abenakis "cultural recognition" by the State Historical Preservation Division, but Governor Howard Dean's administration continued to resist political recognition.

In the spring of 2005, however, despite opposition from the attorney general's office and the threat of a gubernatorial veto, the Vermont Senate unanimously approved a bill, backed by Senator Diane Snelling (R), daughter of the former governor, extending state recognition to the Abenaki people. In November 2005, however, the Bureau of Indian Affairs denied the Abenaki petition for *federal* recognition. With the "threat" of federal recognition apparently removed, the Vermont attorney general's office withdrew much of its opposition, and the bill for state recognition passed the house of representatives. In May 2006 the Vermont Abenakis' state recognition was made official in a bill-signing on the statehouse steps. Abenakis in the twentieth and twenty-first centuries have had to stand up and say to all who would listen, and to those who would not, that they are still living on their own land and that they are a sovereign people. They've been doing it since the eighteenth century.

Western political traditions depict sovereignty as a robust, all or nothing kind of thing. But in America, the founding fathers established government with a system of checks and balances, and Thomas Jefferson said that sovereignty in an absolutist sense was "an idea belonging to the other side of the Atlantic."[35] Even there the queen of England is a sovereign without real power. Sovereignty is not an absolute thing: it can be shared and limited. As the history of the Scottish parliament demonstrates, it is more easily submerged than extinguished. In the Treaty of Union in 1707, Scotland was "bought and sold for English gold," the Scottish parliament merged with the English parliament at Westminster, and Scotland became a very junior partner in a greater Britain. Since 1999, however, Scotland has had its own parliament again. Scots were careful with their phraseology: after a hiatus of almost three hundred years, the new parliament "reconvened." The incorporation of Native peoples into the state is often seen as synonymous with the extinguishment of Native rights and nationhood.[36] But aboriginal rights endure, treaty rights remain, and Scotland has not disappeared; it is, to use a familiar phrase, "a nation within a nation."

Wealth and Poverty

Indian poverty, like the United States, is a relatively recent creation, and there are signs it is on the way out. Tribes are rebuilding their economies, but it takes time to adjust to the loss of 97 percent of America and to untangle the sinews of colonialism. Economic development is fundamental to self-determination, and, as the Harvard Project on American Indian Economic Development has demonstrated, self-determination is fundamental to sustained tribal economic development.[37] Some people ask how tribes can be sovereign if they are dependent on "hand-outs" from the federal government. Other nations that have accepted assistance from the U.S. government or from anyone else would not likely agree that doing so compromised their sovereign status, but Indian poverty apparently renders people dependent politically as well as economically. In many people's minds, Indians and poverty are synonymous terms. Government reports and travelers' accounts documented instances of starvation in Indian communities in the nineteenth century. In the twentieth century, statistics placed reservation communities at the wrong end of every social and economic indicator.

There are different figures, however, from casino communities, and from less spectacular, nongaming tribal enterprises. According to a report issued in February 2005, 223 tribes operate forty-one casinos in twenty-eight states, and Indian gaming pulled in $18.5 billion in 2004. The Indian gaming industry created more than half a million jobs, mostly for non-Indians, and generated $5.5 billion in federal taxes in 2004.[38] (As sovereign nations, tribes are exempt from state and local taxes.) The fact that some tribes have made a killing, takes them out of the "poor Indian" category, which for many people is the only category: the only Indian is a poor Indian. The very fact that they are wealthy means that the Mashantucket Pequots and Mohegans in Connecticut cannot be "real Indians." Even if they "qualify" as Indians culturally or genetically, critics assert, casino tribes have "sold out"; they have bought into the vices of modern society and generate profit in ways and in quantities that are not only "un-Indian" but also do not entail real work. In the case of the Mashantucket Pequots, investigative journalism focuses on the underside of tribal reconstruction and tribal business and politics and points out the irony in "becoming American millionaires by becoming American Indians."[39]

Survival as a business may not be the same thing as surviving as a tribe, but historically there is nothing "un-Indian" about prosperity. The perpetual poverty stereotype is based on postcontact conditions and observations, when economic systems that had functioned effectively for thousands of years no longer worked. Instead, land loss, environmental degradation, the slaughter of game, the inroads of an alien and aggressive market economy, relocation, confinement on reservations, the assaults of alcoholism and other diseases, policies designed to render tribes dependent on government rations, and cumbersome bureaucracies that restricted tribal initiatives prevented recovery. Before contact, Cahokia was a prosperous midcontinent medieval metropolis and trade center; ancestral Pueblos built thriving communities at Chaco Canyon and other locations; and the Pequots were wealthy and powerful in seventeenth-century Connecticut as well as in late-twentieth-century Connecticut—then, they controlled the wampum trade. In the eighteenth century, Mandans and Hidatsas on the Upper Missouri grew rich trading corn; Columbia River peoples grew rich trading salmon; Cheyennes and Comanches became prosperous on the buffalo-rich Great Plains and operated successful exchange networks. Trade systems carried prestige items as well as functional products across hundreds of miles. Native American and European ideas about wealth and how it was used certainly differed, but there was plenty of it.

Indian gaming—and non-Indian complaints about it—is not new either. Daniel Gookin said that Indians in seventeenth-century New England were "addicted to gaming" and would "play away all they have." In the nineteenth century, Hudson Bay Company governor George Simpson said all Indians on the eastern slopes of the Rockies had a "deeply seated" love of gambling, and other traders agreed. Trader John McLean witnessed an all-night stick gambling session, from which players emerged with "their hair disheveled, their eyes bloodshot, and faces ghastly pale," and sometimes with nothing left to cover their nakedness except an old blanket. No matter how bad their luck, they never resorted to suicide, McLean noted, although they did on occasion shoot the winner. Missing the deeper social and economic functions of gaming, traders associated it with idleness. Indians who sat around smoking and gambling, or who bet on racing horses, were not profitably employed hunting beaver pelts for the trade.[40] Wagering on stick games or horse races bears little relation to modern bingo halls and casinos. These are "white institutions that Indians appropriated" and adapted to their own purposes. But, again, Indians have been doing that since first contacts.

Culture and Identity

Casino wealth alone cannot protect Indian cultures and values, of course, and time is running out. Native languages are disappearing at an alarming rate. Each generation seems to be less connected to the ways of their grandparents, and Disney and MTV threaten to finish what the boarding schools started. Everywhere in Indian country, individuals and communities deal with the legacies of colonial education policies that sought to remake Indian students in the white man's image, to eradicate Native languages, and prepare Indian people for a future of assimilation and disappearance. In the late twentieth century, language immersion programs and tribal colleges began to restore some of what was lost. Tribal colleges have succeeded where federal education policies and mainstream colleges failed. They integrate Native American traditions into their curriculum, providing classes in tribal languages, art, philosophy, and history and recognize that reconnecting to these longstanding cultural skills and beliefs gives Indian students confidence to participate in the dominant society. The tribal colleges have received considerable praise—not much funding but considerable praise—and well they should.[41]

Basing education on Indian values is not new, of course; the very first educational systems on the continent did that.

The Onondaga orator Canasatego's famous "thanks but no thanks" response in 1744 to Virginia's offer to educate Iroquois young men free at colonial colleges was but one of many insistencies by Indian people that they be left free to live their own lives, teach their own children, and instill their own values. Oneida headmen rejected Dartmouth's efforts to recruit their sons: "English schools we do not approve of here, as serviceable to our spiritual interest," they said; "almost all those who have been instructed in English are a reproach to us."[42] Canasatego and the Oneidas knew that Indian ways of learning and knowing offered different understandings of the world and that controlling the education of one's young people was a key component of sovereignty. So did Richard Henry Pratt and other educators who tried to eradicate Indian ways and impose American education in their boarding schools.

Identity issues complicate and muddle struggles for cultural survival. As Indian population rose dramatically in the late twentieth century so did conflicts about identity and culture. The Cherokee Nation has more than 175,000 enrolled members, but what it means to be Cherokee can be a controversial and divisive issue, involving notions about blood, race, color and culture.[43] The 2000 census acknowledged demographic realities and recognized that many Indian people, like many other people, have concentric identities. Yet the identity criteria applied by the federal government seem to point to an inevitable erosion of "Indianness." If intermarriage continues as it has for centuries, the number of Indians with one-half or more Indian ancestry will continue to drop dramatically. As historian Patricia Limerick and others have pointed out, if the federal government holds steadily to 25 percent Indian blood quota as the criterion for Indian identity, "eventually Indians will be defined out of existence."[44] But Indians having mixed ancestry, or even having no Indian ancestry, is not a new phenomenon. White captives sometimes were adopted into Indian communities and "turned Indian." The most prominent Abenaki chief at the time of the American Revolution was Joseph Louis Gill, the son of English parents who had been captured by the Abenakis, were adopted into Abenaki society, and raised their son as an Abenaki. "Blood" does not seem to have been an issue. Alexander McGillivray had a Scottish father and a Creek mother but chose the Creek path. John Ross was "seven-eighths Scottish" but was principal chief of the Cherokees. Commitment to community and culture seem to have been much more important than "blood," which should not seem strange to anyone has gone through the process of becoming a U.S. citizen—one need not have "American" blood, but one must absolutely subscribe to the values the United States claims as its own.

Critics say that while powwow culture flourishes, "authentic" Indian culture declines. As elsewhere in the world, "invented traditions" are portrayed as spurious.[45] But there has rarely been a clear-cut contest between "old and new," "traditional and authentic," "modern and invented." Cultures survive by changing, not by standing still. Eighteenth-century Indians embraced many European commodities but kept other aspects of European culture at arm's length. Despite the revelations of the master of life to the Delaware prophet Neolin in the early 1760s and to the Shawnee prophet Tenskwatawa forty years later, Indians were not less Indians because they adopted new technology—bows and arrows in the eighth century, horses and guns in the seventeenth and eighteenth centuries, computers and cell phones in the twentieth century. Are people not who they say they are if they adopt things that other people, or even they themselves, feel are not authentic? New England Indians in the early twentieth century adopted Plains Indian headdresses and buckskins as a regalia of identity, reinforcing their claim to be "still here" to a white audience that had clear, if wrongheaded, ideas of what Indians were supposed to look like. When Creek chief Waldo McIntosh attended his Highland clan's gathering in Scotland in 1964, he wore Plains Indian regalia and had his photo taken next to the clan chief, who dressed in the supposed regalia of an ancient Highlander—tartan kilt, bonnet, sporran. Neither chief wore what their eighteenth-century ancestors would have worn, but they wore important markers of identity, for both wearer and audience.

Writing in 1941 while German bombs rained down on England, George Orwell wondered what his country would be like after the war. There would surely be many profound changes, he concluded, "but England will still be England, an everlasting animal stretching into the future and the past, and, like all living things, having the power to change out of recognition and yet remain the same."[46] What is true for the English nation is surely true for Indian nations. One of my students wrote several years ago, "The United States' policies of assimilating Indians have failed—and will always fail because we will always find new ways of being Indian."[47]

Empires come and go. Peoples and cultures change and survive. History works in cycles. Issues like competition for scarce resources and environmental degradation in the American West, or waging "just and lawful wars authorized by Congress" with conviction that our values and construction of the world are right, are reruns on a larger scale: we've been there before. But to recognize these things we must know our history, and our history must include Indians. Without Indians America has a short history, not much to learn from—and that's the way some people like it. If we don't look beyond yesterday we can kid ourselves that tomorrow too will be bright and sunny. We live in a society where history seems to be valued primarily as entertainment or as providing prestige heritage, where history courses are not mandatory as an integral part of our young people's (or even our teachers') education, and where the government and its media try, in Said's words, to control "the power to narrate, [and] to block other narratives from forming and emerging."[48] Simon Schama writes that "history is the enemy of tyranny, oblivion its greatest accomplice."[49] Monopolizing the telling of history is a potent weapon and historians need to resist it, as Indian people have done for generations.

In the end, the problem is not that Indians suffer from too much history; it is that the United States suffers from too little history and from too few histories. The best remedy is to incorporate the deep histories of Indian America into the national narratives, or better still to incorporate the national narrative into the deep histories of this continent. Those histories will certainly help us to understand the Native

American present; they may also help us to understand our American future because the past, in many ways, is the present. Scottish journalist Neal Ascherson recalls a proverb that illuminates the essential link of past and present, change and continuity, in Indian America as much as in the Highlands of Scotland: "This is my grandfather's axe. My father gave it a new handle. I gave it a new head."[50]

Notes

1. Edward W. Said, paraphrasing T. S. Eliot, wrote, "Past and present inform each other, each implies the other and . . . each coexists with the other." *Culture and Imperialism* (New York: Vintage, 1994), 4.

2. Colin G. Calloway, "Why Did the Anasazi All Live in National Parks?: Indian Histories, Hemispheric Contexts, and 'American Beginnings,'" *William and Mary Quarterly* 58 (July 2001): 703–11.

3. Thanks to my colleague Dan Runnels for this observation.

4. Charles Wilkinson presents a recent and accessible survey of developments in Indian country over the last half century in *Blood Struggle: The Rise of Modern Indian Nations* (New York: W. W. Norton, 2005).

5. Said, *Culture and Imperialism*, 9.

6. John Borrows, *Recovering Canada: The Resurgence of Indigenous Law* (Toronto: University of Toronto Press, 2002), 146.

7. Devon A. Mihesuah, *Natives and Academics: Researching and Writing about American Indians* (Lincoln: University of Nebraska Press, 1998).

8. Francis Paul Prucha, ed., *Documents of United States Indian Policy* (Lincoln: University of Nebraska Press, 1975), 10, 22–23.

9. Donald L. Fixico, *The Invasion of Indian Country in the Twentieth Century: American Capitalism and Tribal Natural Resources* (Niwot: University Press of Colorado, 1998).

10. Marjane Ambler, *Breaking the Iron Bonds: Indian Control of Energy Development* (Lawrence: University of Kansas Press, 1990).

11. E.g., Allan Van Gestal, "The New York Indian Land Claims: The Modern Landowner as Hostage," in *Iroquois Land Claims,* ed. Christopher Vecsey and William A. Starna (Syracuse: Syracuse University Press, 1988), 123–39.

12. Wilkinson, *Blood Struggle*, 266–67.

13. *Federal Power Commission v. Tuscarora Indian Nation*, 362 U.S. 99 at 142.

14. The proclamation is reprinted in Adam Shortt and Arthur G. Doughty, eds., *Documents Relating to the Constitutional History of Canada, 1759–1791,* 2 vols. (Ottawa: Historical Documents Publication Board, 1918), 1:163–68. For discussions, and disagreements about its importance and implications, see L. C. Green and Olive P. Dickinson, *The Law of Nations and the New World* (Edmonton: University of Alberta Press, 1989), 99–124; Robert A. Williams, Jr., *The American Indian in Western Legal Thought: The Discourses of Conquest* (New York: Oxford University Press, 1999), 229; Anthony Pagden, *Lords of All the World: Ideologies of Empire in Spain, Britain, and France, c. 1500–c.1800* (New Haven: Yale University Press, 1995), 85; Gregory Evans Dowd, *War under Heaven: Pontiac, the Indian Nations, and the British Empire* (Baltimore: Johns Hopkins University Press, 2002), 177; John Borrows, "Constitutional Law from a First Nation Perspective: Self-Government and the Royal Proclamation," *UBC Law Review* 28 (1994): 1–47; John Borrows, "Wampum at Niagara: The Royal Proclamation, Canadian Legal History, and Self-Government," in *Aboriginal and Treaty Rights in Canada,* ed. Michael Asche (Vancouver:

University of British Columbia Press, 1997), 155–72; John Borrows, *Recovering Canada*, chap. 5; and Brian Slattery, "The Land Rights of Indigenous Canadian Peoples, as Affected by the Crown's Acquisition of Their Territories" (PhD diss., University of Oxford, 1979).

15. Prucha, *Documents,* 10.

16. Paul Brodeur, *Restitution: The Land Claims of the Mashpee, Passamaquoddy, and Penobscot Indians of New England* (Boston: Northeastern University Press, 1985).

17. Edward Lazarus, *Black Hills/White Justice: The Sioux Nation versus the United States, 1775 to the Present* (New York: HarperCollins, 1991).

18. Fay Cohen, *Treaties on Trial: The Continuing Controversy over Northwest Indian Fishing Rights* (Seattle: University of Washington Press, 1986).

19. For different approaches to treaties, see, e.g., Francis Paul Prucha, *American Indian Treaties: The History of a Political Anomaly* (Berkeley: University of California Press, 1994); Vine Deloria, Jr., and Raymond J. DeMallie, comps., *Documents of American Indian Diplomacy: Treaties, Agreements, and Conventions, 1775–1979,* 2 vols. (Norman: University of Oklahoma Press, 1999); and Bruce E. Johansen, ed., *Enduring Legacies: Native American Treaties and Contemporary Controversies* (Westport, Conn.: Praeger, 2004).

20. Joyce Appleby and Terence Ball, eds., *Jefferson: Political Writings* (Cambridge: Cambridge University Press, 1999), 301.

21. Loron Sauguaarum, "An Account of Negotiations Leading to the Casco Bay Treaty," in *The World Turned Upside Down: Indian Voices from Early America,* ed. Colin G. Calloway (Boston: Bedford Books, 1994), 93.

22. Calloway, *World Turned Upside Down,* 127–28.

23. Armand Francis Lucier, comp., *Pontiac's Conspiracy and Other Indian Affairs: Notices Abstracted from Colonial Newspapers, 1763–1765* (Bowie, Md.: Heritage Books, 2000), 93.

24. Brian Leigh Dunnigan, ed., *Memoir on the Late War in North America between France and England by Pierre Pouchot,* trans. Michael Cardy. (Youngstown, N.Y.: Old Fort Niagara Association, 1994), 57.

25. Clarence Walworth Alvord and Clarence Edwin Carter, eds., *The Critical Period, 1763–1765,* vol. 10 of *Collections of the Illinois State Historical Library* (Springfield: Trustees of the Illinois State Historical Library, 1915), 257–58.

26. Milo M. Quaife, ed., *John Long's Voyages and Travels in the Years 1768–1788* (Chicago: R. R. Donnelley and Sons, 1922), 40.

27. David Jones, *A Journal of Two Visits Made to Some Nations of Indians on the West Side of the River Ohio, in the Years 1772 and 1773* (Burlington, Vt.: Isaac Collins, 1774), 54.

28. Francis Paul Prucha, *American Indian Policy in the Formative Years: The Indian Trade and Intercourse Acts, 1790–1834* (Lincoln: University of Nebraska Press, 1970), 141.

29. *Dred Scott, Plaintiff in error, v. John F. A. Sandford;* Supreme Court of the United States, 60 U.S. 393; 15 L. Ed. 691, December, 1856 Term. I am grateful to Matthew Tso for bringing this aspect of the Dred Scott case to my attention. On the ongoing contest over sovereignty between Indian tribes and the federal government, see David E. Wilkins and K. Tsianina Lomawaima, *Uneven Ground: American Indian Sovereignty and Federal Law* (Norman: University of Oklahoma Press, 2001).

30. Sidney L. Harring, *Crow Dog's Case: American Indian Sovereignty, Tribal Law, and United States Law in the Nineteenth Century* (Cambridge: Cambridge University Press, 1994).

31. David E. Wilkins, *American Indian Sovereignty and the U.S. Supreme Court: The Masking of Justice* (Austin: University of Texas Press, 1997), 67–81.

32. Blue Clark, *Lone Wolf v. Hitchcock: Treaty Rights and Indian Law at the End of the Nineteenth Century* (Lincoln: University of Nebraska Press, 1994).

33. Governor Snelling's quotation is in Bill Weinberg, "Unquiet Earth in Abenaki Country," *Native Americas* 19 (Spring/Summer 2002), which also provides a convenient overview of these issues. Atiwanto in Calloway, *World Turned Upside Down*, 128.

34. *State of Vermont v. Raleigh Elliott, et al.,* No. 90-512; Supreme Court of Vermont, 159 Vt. 102; 616 A. 2d 210; 1992 Vt. LEXIS 122.

35. Qtd. in Wilkinson, *Blood Struggle,* 248.

36. Dale Turner, *This Is Not a Peace Pipe: Towards a Critical Indigenous Philosophy* (Toronto: University of Toronto Press, 2005).

37. A listing of the Harvard Project's publications is available at http://www.ksg.harvard.edu/hpaied/pubs.

38. Erica Werner, "Indian Tribes Are Raking in Chips in Their Casinos," reprinted in *Valley News* (White River Junction, Vt.), February 16, 2005.

39. Brett D. Fromson, *Hitting the Jackpot: The Inside Story of the Richest Indian Tribe in History* (New York: Atlantic Monthly Press, 2003), 223. See also Jeff Benedict, *Without Reservation: The Making of America's Most Powerful Indian Tribe and Foxwoods, the World's Largest Casino* (New York: HarperCollins, 2000), and Kim Isaac Eisler, *Revenge of the Pequots* (New York: Simon and Schuster, 2001).

40. Daniel Gookin, "Historical Collections of the Indians in New England," *Collections of the Massachusetts Historical Society* for 1792 (reprinted Towtaid, N.J., 1970), 19; E. E. Rich, ed., *Simpson's 1828 Journey to the Columbia* (Toronto: The Champlain Society, 1947), 205–206; W. S. Wallace, ed., *John McLean's Notes of a Twenty-Five Years' Service in the Hudson's Bay Territory* (Toronto: The Champlain Society, 1932), 180–81; Elizabeth Vibert, *Traders' Tales: Narratives of*

Cultural Encounters in the Columbia Plateau, 1807–1846 (Norman: University of Oklahoma Press, 1997), 140–44.

41. The Carnegie Foundation for the Advancement of Teaching, *Tribal Colleges: Shaping the Future of Native America* (Princeton, N.J.: Carnegie Foundation for the Advancement of Teaching, 1992).

42. Canasatego's reply and the Oneidas' rejection are in Calloway, *World Turned Upside Down,* 66–68, 101–104; an extended version of Canasatego's response, recorded and likely elaborated by Benjamin Franklin, is in Leonard Labaree, ed., *The Papers of Benjamin Franklin,* 37 vols. (New Haven: Yale University Press, 1959–). See also Red Jacket's famous speech to the Boston Missionary Society, reprinted in Peter Nabokov, ed., *Native American Testimony* (New York: Penguin, 1992), 57.

43. Circe Sturm, *Blood Politics: Race, Culture, and Identity in the Cherokee Nation of Oklahoma* (Berkeley: University of California Press, 2002).

44. Russell Thornton, *American Indian Holocaust and Survival: A Population History since 1492* (Norman: University of Oklahoma Press, 1987), 236–37; Patricia Nelson Limerick, *The Legacy of Conquest: The Unbroken Past of the American West* (New York: W. W. Norton, 1987), 338; Ward Churchill "The Crucible of American Indian Identity: Native Tradition versus Colonial Imposition in Postconquest North America," in *Contemporary Native American Cultural Issues,* ed. Duane Champagne (Walnut Creek, Calif.: Altamira Press, 1999), 39–67.

45. Eric Hobsbawm and Terence Ranger, eds., *The Invention of Tradition* (Cambridge: Cambridge University Press, 1983).

46. George Orwell, *England Your England and Other Essays* (London: Secker and Warburg, 1953), 224.

47. Melanie Joy Shockley (Dartmouth class of 2006), June 2004; quoted with permission.

48. Said, *Culture and Imperialism*, xiii.

49. Simon Schama, *A History of Britain, Volume 3: The Fate of Empire, 1776–2000* (New York: Hyperion, 2002), 558.

50. Neal Ascherson, *Stone Voices: The Search for Scotland* (New York: Hill and Wang, 2002), 41.

Chapter 2

Moving with the Seasons, Not Fixed in Stone

The Evolution of Native American Identity

R. David Edmunds

On January 25, 1900, Edward Goldberg, the Indian agent at the Quapaw Agency in northeastern Indian Territory, wrote to his superiors in Washington, D.C., defending his performance as Indian agent to the Quapaws, Miamis, Seneca-Cayugas and other tribes under his agency's jurisdiction. Proud of the "advances" that some of the tribal people within his agency were making, he boasted that "progressives" such as Cayuga Amos Reed-Bird were making great strides toward accepting the government's ongoing "civilization" program. Nine years earlier, in 1891, Reed-Bird had accepted an allotment near the Neosho River, and unlike some of his kinsmen who continued to travel back and forth between the Seneca-Cayuga community in Indian Territory and Cayuga settlements in both New York and Ontario, Reed-Bird resided permanently on his allotment. He raised pigs and chickens, grazed two horses, and periodically harvested small crops of corn and hay. He also buttressed his income through odd jobs for neighboring non-Indian farmers.

As a boy, Reed-Bird had spoken only Cayuga, and he and his wife still spoke it at home, but he had attended grammar school for four years and could read and write English as well as most of the non-Indian farmers in Indian Territory. Reed-Bird and his family dressed in clothing similar to their white neighbors. Their diet also resembled that of other rural Oklahomans, although they relied more heavily on fish caught from the Neosho River and upon berries and wild greens gathered in the river bottoms. Reed-Bird sent his children to the government school, but like many other Oklahomans of his time, he kept them home when the weather was bad or when extra hands were needed for the chores on his allotment.

A respected member of the Seneca-Cayuga community, Reed-Bird sat on the Cayuga council, and he also led in the festivities surrounding the tribe's annual Green Corn Ceremony, held in the tribal longhouse each August. Although Indian Agent Goldberg had attempted to discourage the Seneca-Cayugas from participating in such traditional ceremonies, he had met with little success. The celebrations continued year after year, and by 1900 Goldberg admitted that they seemed harmless enough, particularly when compared to the new peyote faith that seemed to be spreading across Indian Territory. Like many other Indian agents, Goldberg was confused and uncertain about the new religion, but it seemed to threaten the government's authority. Both bureaucrats and missionaries had been hard pressed to eradicate the old tribal beliefs; they did not welcome any new indigenous religions that might replace them.[1]

Yet Goldberg remained optimistic. If Reed-Bird or other tribespeople seemed interested in peyote, they also were eager to embrace American technology. To the agent's surprise, Reed-Bird and several other Seneca-Cayuga tribal council members had pooled their resources and purchased a small, open motor car that Reed-Bird or other council members periodically piloted along the dirt roads that crossed the region. Reed-Bird also delighted in providing rides to tribal children on Sundays and at tribal gatherings, where he also instructed the children in Seneca-Cayuga tribal traditions.

As he concluded his report, Goldberg confidently assured officials in Washington that their Indian policies were achieving success. Progressives like Amos Reed-Bird were literate in English, now dressed in "white-man's" clothing, resided on their own allotments, and even drove new-fangled automobiles. "Civilized ways" were coming to Indian Territory.

A century later, Reed-Bird's great-grandson, Thomas Red-Bird (the surname had been changed when a principal at the Seneca Boarding School had first inadvertently misspelled the name, then refused to admit his mistake) sat drinking coffee in the community hall at the Seneca-Cayuga tribal complex in Miami, Oklahoma. Red-Bird was seated across the table from his sister-in-law Elsie Reynolds, and they had been discussing the tribal council's decision to pursue land claims in upstate New York. Elsie approved of the policies, but Red-Bird was less certain.[2]

Red-Bird had been born in 1937, still resided on his family's diminished allotment near modern Grove, Oklahoma, and continued to subscribe to a series of cultural patterns that resembled those of his great-grandfather. Like his great-grandfather, he also farmed a few acres, harvesting hay that he fed to his three horses. He drove a battered pick-up truck between his home and a marina on nearby Lake of the Cherokees, where he worked part-time as a general handyman, and as a fishing guide when customers were available. Like many other Native American men in rural Oklahoma, Red-Bird regularly wore cowboy boots, jeans, and western shirts, although he had replaced his worn Stetson with a baseball cap bearing the Seneca-Cayuga tribal logo.[3]

Red-Bird spoke English in his home, but like his great-grandfather, he retained a good knowledge of the Cayuga language (he was one of less than two dozen tribe members who still possessed this fluency), and he was disappointed that his children, and particularly his grandchildren, seemed to have little interest in learning the Cayuga tongue. Red-Bird was a respected member of the Seneca-Cayuga community, and like his great-grandfather, he served as a "pot-hanger," or ceremonial leader, at the tribe's annual Green Corn Ceremony. He also served as the source of considerable tribal oral tradition, and both tribe members and interested outsiders often relied upon him to answer their questions regarding tribal traditions. Although the Native American Church had few adherents among the Seneca-Cayugas, Red-Bird had become a member, often driving many miles to attend ceremonies among the Pawnees, who resided near modern Pawnee and Skeedee, Oklahoma.[4]

During the 1970s Red-Bird had served on the Seneca-Cayuga tribal council, but more recently he had become increasingly critical of the organization. Although he realized that modern Native American people needed to pursue employment in the non-Indian world, and he himself worked at the marina, he opposed many of entrepreneurial activities championed by the current tribal council. Investments in smoke shops, gas stations, and convenience stores were bad enough, but Red-Bird was particularly opposed to the tribe's bingo facility and the council's attempts to expand their gaming enterprises into other locations. He feared that exposure to new economic endeavors, and the potential financial returns that such activities might engender, could potentially alter the nature of the Seneca-Cayuga community. He remembered the good times of his youth. In the 1940s and 1950s, the Seneca-Cayuga people often had struggled to make ends meet, but their lives seemed more focused on the old sense of community. Now things seemed to be changing too quickly. Red-Bird knew that although many of the younger tribe members supported the changes, they still respected him for his knowledge of tribal traditions and language; but they now considered him to be a "traditional" elder, a respected senior adviser, but dedicated to older ways. Red-Bird sipped the last of the coffee from his heavy porcelain cup and stared out the doorway of the dining hall toward the tribe's gaming annex. Hmphh! Well, maybe he was "traditional," but from his perspective, the council needed to "slow down." Not all new and "progressive" ideas were good ones.[5]

Although Indian agent Edward Goldberg actually served at the Quapaw Agency and the circumstances surrounding the Seneca-Cayuga community are based upon historical events, both Amos Reed-Bird and Thomas Red-Bird are fictitious, composite characters based on Seneca-Cayuga history and culture.[6] The point, however, is that the two Seneca-Cayuga men subscribed to very similar values and cultural patterns, but during the twentieth century Seneca-Cayuga culture, like tribal cultures elsewhere, continued to evolve. Within the contexts of their times, the two men exemplified very different positions on the admittedly arbitrary, but widely accepted, spectrum of Native American adaptation. Fluent in English and possessing the rudiments of a frontier education, Amos Reed-Bird was described as "progressive" and "making great strides toward civilization" because he lived on his allotment, attempted yeoman agriculture, worked within the non-Indian employment market, and even drove a motor vehicle. A century later, things had changed. Reed-Bird's great-grandson, Thomas Red-Bird, subscribed to a similar lifestyle. He resided on his allotment, raised hay and horses, worked part-time for non-Indians, and drove a truck. He too spoke fluent Cayuga and was knowledgeable in regard to Seneca-Cayuga history and ceremonies; but Red-Bird was seen as "traditional" by many modern Seneca-Cayugas, who now possessed more formal education, did not speak Cayuga, worked full-time in neighboring Miami, Tulsa, or Joplin Missouri, and supported the tribal council's efforts to expand business enterprises and gaming. Obviously, during the twentieth century (as in previous eras) Seneca-Cayuga culture, and what it meant to be Seneca-Cayuga, had continued to evolve. As Amanda Bearskin Greenback, a Seneca-Cayuga tribal elder recently stated, Seneca-Cayuga people (like all Native American people) always have "moved with the seasons." Cayuga identity continues, but it has never been fixed in stone.[7]

At the beginning of the twentieth-first century, Native American identity, or "being Indian," faces some significant challenges. Questions continue to emerge as to definitions, particularly as to how the parameters of tribal membership are to be determined. Should enrollment in federally recognized tribes remain the sole criteria through which Native American, Native, indigenous, or Indian people are defined? Each tribal government now has the legal right to determine that tribe's membership, and the spectrum of this determination varies from tribe to tribe. To my knowledge, all the tribes in Oklahoma rely on the principle of biological descent, but minimal blood quantum limits differ markedly from tribe to tribe. A recent survey of twenty-five tribal enrollment offices indicates that some tribes require that enrolled members possess a tribal blood quantum ranging from one quarter to one-sixteenth. But there are growing and notable exceptions. The Five Southern Tribes, in addition to most other tribal governments in the eastern half of the state, also rely on biological descent, but all except the Creeks (who still require one-eighth lineage) have abandoned the blood quantum requirements.[8] Of course, the irony of all of this is that the concept of blood quantum is not a Native American one but was originated by the federal government. Blood quantums first appeared on removal lists when Indian agents enrolled the eastern tribes for removal to lands west of the Mississippi. Many of these newcomers to Indian Territory retained the blood quantum records during the territorial period, and the government then extended these criteria to other tribes who were allotted under the Dawes Act. Following the allotment period, the tribes' reliance on blood quantums became commonplace.[9]

But is a specific blood quantum a viable measure of tribal membership? The answer remains unclear. Undoubtedly, for the foreseeable future, all tribes will rely on some degree of biological descent, but as Native American people continue to intermarry with non-Indians, the blood quantum of tribal members will predictably decline. Currently, over half of all Native American people live in large urban areas, and within that urban Indian population, about 60 percent of young Native American women of "marrying age" will marry non-Indians. Indeed, in 1980 over half of all American Indians already were married to non-Indians. A far greater proportion of these lived in urban areas, but since the proportion of Native American people living in cities now also exceeds one half and continues to increase, the rate of intermarriage undoubtedly also will accelerate. Cherokee demographer Russell Thornton has pointed out that in 1980 about 87 percent of the Native American population possessed a blood quantum of at least 50 percent, but if current trends continue, by 2080 that number will shrink from 87 percent to 8 percent. Moreover, the percentage of people with less than a one-quarter blood quantum is projected to increase from about 4 percent in 1980 to almost 60 percent by the middle decades of the twenty-first century. Obviously, as this phenomenon proliferates, tribes will be forced to adjust their blood quantum requirements, or they will legislate themselves out of existence. Tribes whose members continue to reside primarily in rural reservation communities are just beginning to face this problem, but it certainly looms in their future. The number of "full-bloods" on almost all tribal rolls continues to decline.[10]

Yet the reliance upon descent as the primary criteria in defining Native American identity may, in itself, raise questions:

Are other factors, such as adherence to generally accepted cultural patterns, more important than biological lineage in ascertaining who really is functioning as a member of a tribal community? Can an individual adopted into a tribal community, and his or her descendants, be defined as part of the tribe? Certainly we know that historically, prior to the twentieth century, such was often the case. Individuals from other tribes, or non-Indians for that matter, often were integrated into tribal communities; they became, for all practical purposes, full-fledged, accepted members of the tribe.[11]

Today these types of adoptions cause considerable controversy. Regardless of the adoptee's adherence to accepted norms of tribal behavior, they often are not official members of the tribe. Before accepting my current position at the University of Texas at Dallas, I served on the faculty of a large university in the Midwest. That institution received an application for admission into its graduate program from an individual living on a reservation on the northern plains. He was not of Native American ancestry but as a child had been legally adopted by a couple who both were members of the tribe. He had grown up in the tribal community, was versed in tribal traditions, took part in many tribal ceremonies, and was one of perhaps ten or twelve fluent speakers of the tribal language. When he was in his early twenties, his adopted father died, and as an expression of his grief, he severed part of a finger (a traditional method of mourning among the tribe in the nineteenth-century). He subsequently applied to the university and sought financial assistance through the institution's minority recruitment program but was informed by university officials that he was ineligible since he was not officially a member of the tribe and consequently was (legally) not an Indian. He eventually enrolled in another institution, but his rejection by the Midwestern university vividly illustrates the conflict between differing definitions of Native American identity based upon blood quantums and adherence to cultural values of tribal communities.

So if both cultural patterns and blood quantum percentages have evolved over the twentieth century, what will be the future of Native American identity? Will it be the same in Oklahoma as in other places? No one can be sure, but some patterns seem obvious. Recently, some academics have written about the emergence of "urban Indians," individuals or groups claiming Native American descent but reticent or unwilling to claim any tribal affiliation: individuals "far from their indigenous forbearers' various homelands, Indians [who] have found each other and created new Indian communities, partly by sharing stories from their respective tribal pasts and partly by making their own urban experiences into a shared Indian story."[12] Sociologists refer to this phenomenon as "Indianess on the supratribal level," an ethnicity that may not completely replace tribal identities but that "encompasses and supplements them."[13]

Undoubtedly Native American people living in large urban areas often band together, and they face problems different from those who continue to reside on reservations or near tribal offices and homelands, but as Susan Harjo recently pointed out in *Indian Country Today,* urban Indians who are reluctant to reveal their tribal affiliation should be suspect, particularly if they have used their projected ethnicity for personal gain. It is difficult to believe that such a claim would be taken seriously in Oklahoma, where almost all Native

American people are within easy driving distance of their tribal offices. Moreover, it is difficult to imagine that any Native American person would claim to be Native American and deprecate their tribal affiliation. Even unenrolled but legitimate tribally descended people's first claim invariably is to a tribal entity, not to the much more ambiguous claim of "being Indian."[14]

In Oklahoma (as in most other places in the United States) some form of biological descent from a state or federally recognized tribe undoubtedly will continue to play the trump card in ascertaining tribal identity, but for most tribes, the blood quantum limitation will either markedly decline or be eliminated. Indeed, conversations with tribal enrollment agents indicate that since growing numbers of current tribal members' children currently are ineligible for enrollment, most tribes who still retain a one-quarter minimal blood quantum now are reconsidering their requirements. Some tribes have attempted to increase blood quantums, and others oppose lowering blood quantum restrictions for economic reasons, but they seem to be swimming against a rising tide of intermarriage that is unlikely to ebb.[15]

If biological descent in some form remains a criterion for both tribal and Native American identity in the twenty-first century, what cultural patterns will future Native Americans embrace? Will certain facets of modern Native American existence be privileged and singled out for protection and retention? Such probably will be the case. Foremost among these institutions will be a tribal land base. During the twentieth century those tribes who continued to possess reservations have assiduously defended them, and the handful of tribes who lost their reservations through the termination policies of the 1950s have endeavored, with some success, to have those reservation lands restored. In Oklahoma, tribes who held minimal acreages of land in the 1950s have steadily increased their holdings until many now have considerable lands in federal trust. The classic case is the Citizen Potawatomi Nation, who in the late 1950s owned only 2.5 acres and warehoused all their tribal records in a garden shed in one member's backyard. Through hard work and dedicated leadership, the Citizen Potawatomis now own 1,200 acres in modern Pottawatomie County, Oklahoma. Although most other tribal governments in Oklahoma have not increased their acreages as exponentially, they certainly have added to their land bases.[16]

Why are these tribal land bases important? Because they remain the well-spring of tribal identity and enterprise. Just as many tribespeople on the northern plains, intermountain region, and desert southwest consider their reservations to be "home" and, if they are not permanent residents, return regularly for ceremonies, homecomings, or family gatherings, so Native Americans in Oklahoma also return regularly to tribal or ceremonial centers to reaffirm their sense of community and to meet with family members and friends. Kenneth McIntosh, the grandson of Chief W. E. "Dode" McIntosh, has referred to the Creek stomp dance held regularly across the old Creek homeland as the "heartbeat" of the modern Creek Nation. One only has to attend such a contest at the New Tulsa Stomp Ground near Holdenville, or be present at the Pawnee Indian Veterans Homecoming or the annual Comanche Homecoming near Medicine Park, to appreciate how important tribal land bases are in providing a geographic arena where a sense of tribal identity can be reaffirmed and replenished. Grace Thorpe, a prominent Sauk and Fox tribal elder has admonished future generations, "Hang on to the land. Hang on to the land. Don't give it up." Most tribal people in Oklahoma, as elsewhere, have continued to heed her advice.[17]

Yet tribal land bases offer more than spiritual replenishment. Since the passage of the Indian Self-Determination and Education Act of 1975, the liberalization of state gaming laws in the 1970s, and the Reagan administration's adoption of a "new federalism" in the 1980s, tribal governments have enlarged both tribal sovereignty and its accompanying economic envelope to provide a broad spectrum of both services and business opportunities for tribal communities. Gaming is the most widely publicized facet of this recent phenomenon. Yet it has proven more successful in some locations than in others and is not the panacea that some of its promoters claim. More important is the unique status of reservation or tribally owned land to lure industrial development and to market commodities such as tobacco and gasoline free from state or local taxes. Hopefully, funds generated from gaming or other narrowly focused endeavors can be invested in broader enterprises. John "Rocky" Barrett, Chairman of the Citizen Potawatomi Nation Business Committee, has likened such revenue to seed corn and has reminded Potawatomis that seed corn should be planted not eaten. The Citizen Potawatomis have planted and cultivated their corn well. They now own a bank, a supermarket, and a golf course. Currently they are the largest single employer in Pottawatomie County. In the long run this broader economic activity offers greater promise for economic growth and stability than does gaming, which faces a potentially glutted market and growing competition from a wide range of non-Indian entities.[18]

Regardless of its source, revenue from tribally based enterprises is critical for a tribe's control over its future. Like Thomas Red-Bird, there are individuals in every tribal community who doubt the wisdom of gaming, and there is an ongoing debate over just which economic activities to embrace, but the tribal communities must become economically self-sufficient. Otherwise they will be forced to rely upon the federal government, which during the late nineteenth and much of the twentieth century provided most tribal communities with annuities, some social services, and legal protection. Ironically, however, if there is one thing to be learned from an examination of the history of Indian-white relations during this period, it is that, very often when push comes to shove, the federal government cannot be relied upon. Throughout American history when tribal communities have possessed anything that non-Indians wanted (land, water, lumber, fish and game, or even children), they have taken it. Both state and federal governments in the United States remain vulnerable to influence by powerful pressure groups. These groups have access to considerable financial resources. If tribal communities hope to defend themselves, they also must assemble sufficient capital.

These resources also can be used to protect those facets of tribal culture that the communities hope to preserve, protect, or even develop. Obviously, both tribal cultures and Native American identity will continue to evolve, but in addition to tribal land bases, there seems to be general consensus that tribes should do their best to retain and propagate tribal languages. Some tribes currently have no members still fluent in their native languages, and in other tribes the community of speakers already has shrunk below the critical mass that linguists argue is necessary for a language to continue. Even relatively isolated tribal communities who still possess a sufficient nucleus of fluency (Navajos, Lakotas, Ojibwes, etc.) now find themselves bombarded by modern electronic media that threatens more than just tribal languages. Still, many tribes have channeled part of their newly generated resources into formal language programs designed to preserve tribal languages and provide their children with language enrichment programs in tribally based schools. Admittedly, for many tribal communities, this will be an uphill battle, but some gains are being made. Colleges and universities are now offering formal instruction in tribal languages for teachers or other individuals who will serve in the communities, and linguists have recorded and produced extensive teaching materials in languages ranging from Arikara to Cherokee. In Mississippi the Choctaws have used the profits from their tribally based Chahta Enterprises to purchase a local television station that broadcasts daily in Choctaw, providing newscasts, children's shows, and programs as diverse as advice on personal finance and microwave cooking. More than 80 percent of Mississippi Choctaws are now fluent in their language.[19]

Undoubtedly, as both tribal cultures and identities evolve, communities, either separately or together, will use their resources to protect or nurture other things that they treasure. The passage of the Native American Graves Protection and Repatriation Act (NAGPRA) in 1990 addressed the desecration of Native American graves and the disposition of human remains, grave goods, and other associated items, but similar issues remain and will continue to confront tribal people. At the present, many tribes believe that special places, sites not associated with graves or human remains but having a particular religious or historical significance to tribal communities, are endangered by either the ignorance or callousness of non-Indians and that efforts should be made for their preservation. The proposal in 1994 to transform the site of the Grand Village of the Kickapoos of the Prairie, a rural location in modern McLean County, Illinois, into a large hog lot presents a classic case. At the last minute the site was saved, but tribes will continue to need funds to protect such places. Current contests over sacred and historical sites in the Black Hills (Bear Butte), and in New Mexico (Blue Lake) and Arizona (San Francisco Peaks) offer other examples. If these places are to be protected, the struggle will be expensive. Tribal communities need to develop the resources needed to finance these undertakings.[20]

As the twenty-first century unfolds, there will be many other issues that will attract Native American attention and resources, and an essay of this length is not the venue to speculate about, or explore all of them. But there is at least one other issue that will remain critical if tribal people wish to maintain control over their land bases and their ability to adapt to changes that undoubtedly will occur. They will continue to need well-educated, highly skilled Native American people to confront and manage these issues. During the last quarter-century, considerable progress has been made. In the mid-1970s, I left the University of Oklahoma to accept a teaching position at the University of Wyoming. At that time the ranks were so small that I knew almost every other academic of Native American descent in U.S. higher education, at least in the arts and humanities. Since that time the number has increased to such an extent that, happily, I can no longer make such a claim. Moreover, the increase has not just been limited to academics. During the 1970s I participated in a series of lectures in Wyoming, Colorado, and surrounding states in which materials were presented in regard to Native American land claims, the American Indian Movement, and Native American issues in general. At that time the most frequently asked question from these "town and gown" audiences was what did tribal communities, or Indian people in general, need most to assist them in attaining their goals and protecting their interests. My rather trite reply was "about a thousand young Indian lawyers." Their ranks do not number one thousand, but the emergence of a cadre of highly trained Native American attorneys, as exemplified by those associated with the Native American Rights Fund certainly have made a big difference. In addition, growing numbers of Native American MBAs, accountants, computer scientists, social workers, and medical personnel also have helped to transform and invigorate many tribal communities.

Tribal colleges also have played an important role in this process. In addition to preparing students for admission to four-year colleges or universities, many tribal colleges have developed curricula specifically designed to meet the needs of tribal communities. In many cases, they offer courses and certified programs that provide members of tribal communities with the skills necessary for the labor demands of local economies. Moreover, they also provide language programs and other cultural enrichment courses that strengthen tribal communities. Currently thirty-one colleges (twenty-eight tribally controlled, three federally chartered) spread across twelve states boast an enrollment of almost twenty-seven thousand students.[21]

Oklahoma provides an ideal location for these programs to flourish. In Oklahoma, as nowhere else, Native American people have successfully constructed a way of life that retains many of the cherished traditions of the past, and they have combined these values with educational and economic opportunities to create both modern tribal and pan-tribal societies. Several factors have contributed to this evolution. Ironically, Indian removal may have been one of them. Many of the tribal people who were removed from the East into Indian Territory, while still in their old homelands already had become adept at integrating their traditional tribal ways with the society that surrounded them. For most, the removal process was traumatic, but it also forced the emigrant tribes into a new region, which encouraged their adoption of new ways. These societies evolved in this new land, they provided a catalyst for the evolution of tribal people already living in the region, and both the newcomers and indigenous tribes have continued to evolve throughout the late nineteenth and twentieth centuries. Ironically, the tragic severance of many Oklahoma tribes from their former homelands may have facilitated a cultural evolution that has worked to their advantage.

Indian people in Oklahoma also have had the advantage of access to formal education. Again, some of the tribes had developed rudimentary formal educational systems prior to their removal, and after their relocation this process expanded. Of course, the extent of tribal school systems varied from tribe to tribe, but among the Cherokees and Choctaws it certainly rivaled or surpassed the public school systems of surrounding states such as Arkansas, Texas, or Louisiana. By 1859, for example, almost fifteen hundred students were enrolled at thirty schools throughout the Cherokee Nation; moreover, in 1859 only two teachers in the Cherokee public school system were non-Cherokees. As a result, the literacy rate for the Cherokee Nation surpassed that of the white South, at least through the antebellum period.[22]

And finally, there is no place on earth with more historical or political precedent for a focus upon Native American studies than the University of Oklahoma. Oklahoma, from its territorial beginnings, has a rich history of Native American education. This university is surrounded by one of the most highly educated Native American populations in the United States. The state's license plates and its television ads promoting tourism proclaim that Oklahoma is "Native America." The University of Oklahoma Press has long been a leader among scholarly presses who publish books about Native Americans. With its rich traditions, its access to unequaled Native American historical and cultural resources, and its location amidst a large, relatively well-educated Native American population, the University of Oklahoma educates, serves, and provides information about Native American people. These endeavors should be supported and encouraged. Oklahoma has a unique heritage, but it is not the only state with a substantial Native American population or with a commitment to Indian education. Other state universities have also emerged as allies that tribes can depend on as they face the future.

Access to education, and its associated technology and economic development, has given Native Americans in Oklahoma a "leg up" on some of the more isolated tribal communities. It also has enabled many Indian people in Oklahoma to build lives with meaningful futures. Obviously many of the social and economic problems that beset Indian communities across the United States also have taken root in this state, but most tribal people in Oklahoma look ahead with considerable optimism. Over the past century and a half, "being Indian" in Oklahoma has often encompassed a broader spectrum of blood quantums, cultural activities, and acceptance of change than in many other regions, but Native peoples' sense of Indian identity has never wavered. In Oklahoma as elsewhere, Indian identity has, and will continue to evolve, but Indian identity in Oklahoma, and Oklahoma's racially mixed, relatively well-educated Indian society, as it evolves, may serve as a viable model for many other tribal communities across the nation.[23]

Notes

1. Erminie Wheeler-Voegelin, "The 19th and 20th Century Ethnohistory of Various Groups of Cayuga Indians," 1959, 109–12 (a copy of this report is in the author's possession). Also see expert witness testimony in support of Seneca-Cayuga land claims, R. David Edmunds, "The Origins and History of the Western Band of the Cayuga Indian Nation," 2004, 23 (copy in author's possession).

2. Native American surnames often were changed (sometimes inadvertently, sometimes purposefully) by both missionaries and federal officials. E.g., White Hair, a Potawatomi from the Fox River in northern Illinois, was first mentioned in government records in 1811,

but subsequent federal correspondence listed him as "White Hare." He later was listed as "White Rabbit." Among the Northern Arapahos, the surname Iron Eyes was changed by missionaries to "Goggles." See R. David Edmunds, *The Potawatomis: Keepers of the Fire* (Norman: University of Oklahoma Press, 1978), 176–204 passim; Eugene Goggles, conversation with author, November 9, 1971, Laramie, Wyoming.

3. Mid-twentieth-century and contemporary Seneca-Cayuga life is discussed in James Howard, "Environment and Culture: The Case of the Oklahoma Seneca-Cayuga" (parts 1 and 2), *North Dakota Quarterly* 29, nos. 3 and 4 (1970): 66–71, 113–22.

4. The evolution of Seneca-Cayuga ceremonialism, including the role of the pot-hangers, is discussed in James Howard, "Cultural Persistence and Cultural Change as Reflected in Oklahoma Seneca-Cayuga Ceremonialism," *Plains Anthropologist* 6, no. 11 (1961): 21–30. Also see William C. Sturtevant, "Oklahoma Seneca-Cayuga," in *Handbook of North American Indians: Volume 15, Northeast,* ed. Bruce E. Trigger (Washington: Smithsonian Institution, 1978), 537–43. The peyote faith is discussed at length in Omer C. Stewart, *Peyote Religion: A History* (Norman: University of Oklahoma Press, 1987). Also see Douglas R. Parks, "Pawnee," in *Handbook of North American Indians: Volume 13, Part 1, Plains,* ed. Raymond J. DeMallie (Washington: Smithsonian Institution, 2001), 543.

5. Seneca-Cayuga tribal government and economic activities are briefly described in "Seneca-Cayuga Tribe of Oklahoma," in *Tiller's Guide to Indian Country,* ed. Veronica E. Tiller (Albuquerque: BowArrow, 1996), 533–34. Information regarding Seneca-Cayuga claims to lands in New York, and the tribe's subsequent legal actions, can be found in R. David Edmunds, "The Origins and History of the Western Band of the Cayuga Indian Nation," a legal report prepared for the tribe that remains in the author's possession. Also see *Cayuga Indians of New York et al. v.*

Mario Cuomo et al., United States District Court, Northern District of New York, Civil Nos. 80-CV-930 and 80-CV-960.

6. See "Preliminary Inventory of the Records of the Miami (Quapaw) Indian Agency," National Archives, Record Group 75, Southwest Region, Fort Worth, Texas, December 19, 2003, 2.

7. Amanda Bearskin Greenback, interview, Miami, Oklahoma, January 8, 2004.

8. Telephone interviews, March 22, 2005, with enrollment agents of the following tribes: Absentee Shawnees, Caddos, Cherokees, Cheyenne-Arapahos, Chickasaws, Choctaws, Citizen Potawatomis, Comanches, Creeks, Ft. Sill Apaches, Iowas, Kansas, Kickapoos, Kiowas, Miamis, Osages, Otoe-Missourias, Pawnees, Poncas, Quapaws, Sacs and Foxes, Seminoles, Seneca-Cayugas, Wichitas, Wyandottes. Those tribes with specific blood-quantum requirements are as follows: 1/4, Absentee Shawnees, Cheyenne-Arapahos, Kiowas, and Otoe-Missourias; 1/8, Iowas, Pawnees, Poncas, Sacs and Foxes, and Wichitas; and 1/16, Caddos and Ft. Sill Apaches.

9. For examples of removal rolls containing blood-quantum assessments, see "A Roll of Ottawa, Chippeway and Potawatomi Emigrated Indians . . . under the Direction of Isaac L. Berry," 1838, National Archives, Records of the Bureau of Indian Affairs, Letters Received by the Office of Indian Affairs (M234), Roll 752, 189; "Muster Roll of a Band of Pottawatomie Indians Delivered at the Osage River Agency," October 6, 1840, ibid., Roll 642, 234–36. Also see "A Census of the Cherokee Nation of Indians, 1896" (a copy of this census can be found in the National Archives Depository at the Federal Records Center in Fort Worth, Texas), and "Census of Indians at the Quapaw Agency on June 30, 1913, taken by Ira C. Deaver, Superintendent," Tribal Archives, Seneca-Cayuga Tribe, Miami, Oklahoma. I would like to thank Meg Hacker, director of Archival Operations at the National

Archives and Records Administration-Southwest (Fort Worth), for her assistance in checking tribal census records.

10. Russell Thornton, *American Indian Holocaust and Survival: A Population History since 1492* (Norman: University of Oklahoma Press, 1987), 236–37. Also see Russell Thornton, "Health, Disease, and Demography," in *A Companion to American Indian History,* ed. Philip J. Deloria and Neal Salisbury (Malden, Mass.: Blackwell, 2002), 76–80.

11. The historical literature contains ample references to this phenomenon. E.g., among the Potawatomis, Shabbona, a leading early nineteenth-century chief had been born at Ottawa, while Billy Caldwell, who led the tribe during the removal period was of Irish-Mohawk descent. See Edmunds, *Potawatomis,* 172; and James A. Clifton, "Personal and Ethnic Identity on the Great Lakes Frontier: The Case of Billy Caldwell," *Ethnohistory* 25 (Winter 1978): 69–94. Also see Margaret Schmidt Hacker, *Cynthia Ann Parker: The Life and the Legend* (El Paso: Texas Western Press, 1990); Sarah E. Cooke and Rachel B. Ramadhyani, comps., *Indians and a Changing Frontier: The Art of George Winter* (Indianapolis: Indiana Historical Society, 1993), 133; and Susan Sleeper-Smith, "Resistance to Removal: The 'White Indian' Frances Slocum," in *People of Persistence: Native Americans in the Midwest,* ed. R. David Edmunds (Urbana: University of Illinois Press, forthcoming).

12. Alexandra Harmon, "Wanted: More Histories of Indian Identity," in Deloria and Salisbury, *A Companion,* 254–55.

13. Ned Blackhawk, "I Can Carry on From Here: The Relocation of American Indians to Los Angeles," *Wicaza-sa Review* 11 (Fall 1995): 16–18; Joane Nagel, *American Indian Ethnic Renewal: Red Power and the Resurgence of Identity and Culture* (New York: Oxford University Press, 1997), 137–40.

14. Susan Shown Harjo, "Why Native Identity Matters: A Cautionary Tale," *Indian Country Today,* February 10, 2005.

15. Telephone interviews, March 22, 2005, with enrollment agents of the following tribes: Absentee Shawnees, Kiowas of Oklahoma, Otoe-Missourias. Also see Ronald I. Trosper, "Native American Boundary Maintenance: The Flathead Indian Reservation, Montana, 1860–1970," *Ethnicity* 3 (1976): 256–74.

16. Jeremy Finch, Director of Cultural Resources, Citizen Potawatomi Nation, telephone interview, March 29, 2005. For tribal opposition to termination, and efforts by tribes to reestablish reservations or tribal trust regions see Donald L. Fixico, *Termination and Relocation: Federal Indian Policy, 1945–1960* (Albuquerque: University of New Mexico Press, 1986); and Nicholas C. Peroff, *Menominee Drums: Tribal Termination and Restoration, 1954–1974* (Norman: University of Oklahoma Press, 1982).

17. "Grace Thorpe," in *Always a People: Histories of Contemporary Woodland Indians,* ed. Rita Kohn and Lynwood Montell (Bloomington: Indiana University Press, 1997), 251. Kenneth McIntosh, is the grandson of W. W. "Dode" McIntosh (Tuskenugge Micco), the last appointed chief of the Creek Nation, and the son of Chinnubbie McIntosh (Haccoce), who also has remained active in Creek tribal government. McIntosh, e-mail to author, April 7, 2005; McIntosh, e-mail to author, April 8, 2005 (copies of this correspondence are in the author's possession).

18. For a discussion of the growth of tribal sovereignty and the "new federalism," see Stephen Cornell, *The Return of the Native: American Indian Political Resurgence* (New York: Oxford University Press, 1988), 202–13; Donald Parman, *Indians and the American West in the Twentieth Century* (Bloomington: Indiana University Press, 1994), 175–81. In *Killing the White Man's Indian,* Fergus Bordewich presents an analysis of the ability of the Mississippi Choctaws to utilize the "new federalism" for economic gain. See Bordewich, *Killing the White Man's Indian: Reinventing Native Americans at the End of the Twentieth*

Century (New York: Anchor Books, 1996), 302–11. For a critical analysis of Native American gaming, see Gerald Vizenor, "Gambling," in *Encyclopedia of North American Indians,* ed. Fred E. Hoxie (Boston: Houghton Mifflin, 1996), 212–14. Information regarding Citizen Potawatomi economic enterprise activity comes from a telephone conversation between the author and Jeremy Finch, March 29, 2005.

19. The support for tribal languages is widespread. See, e.g., the interviews with tribal leaders and elders in Kohn and Montell, *Always a People.* Also see Benton R. White and Christine Schultz White, "Philip Martin," in *The New Warriors: Native American Leaders since 1900,* ed. R. David Edmunds (Lincoln: University of Nebraska Press, 2001), 195–209.

20. "After 166 Years, the Kickapoos Come Home: Native People Connect to Illinois Current Inhabitants," *The Pantagraph* (Bloomington, Ill.), May 31, 1998; Brenda Norrell, "Tribes Appeal San Francisco Peaks Decision," *Indian Country Today,* April 3, 2005. Also see Jack F. Trope, "Sacred Sites," in *Native Americans in the Twentieth Century: An Encyclopedia,* ed. Mary B. Davis (New York: Garland, 1996), 564–66.

21. For a good example of an institution focused toward the needs of a tribal community see René Sanchez, "At Little Big Horn, an Outpost of Learning: Tribal Colleges Helping to Revive Tradition of Self-Reliance," *Washington Post,* July 12, 1997, AO1; Bordewich, *Killing the White Man's Indian,* 286–97. Also see Paul Boyer, "Tribal Colleges," in Davis, *Native Americans,* 649–51; and Marjane Ambler, "Tribal Colleges Redefining Success," *Tribal College Journal of American Indian Education* 16, no. 3:8–9; and American Indian Higher Education Consortium, http://www.aihec.org/documents/research/intro (accessed 2003).

22. R. David Edmunds, Frederick Hoxie, and Neal Salisbury, *The People: A History of Native America* (Boston: Houghton-Mifflin, forthcoming), chaps. 9 and 11.

23. For a discussion of the unique evolution of tribal culture and identity among the Five Southern Tribes, see W. David Baird, "Are the Five Tribes of Oklahoma 'Real' Indians?" *Western Historical Quarterly* 21 (February 1990): 6–18.

Chapter 3

Three Stories of War

History and Memory in an American Indian Community

Laurence M. Hauptman

In the academy, the "memory business" has begun to domi-
nate scholarship. Books on memory, collective memory,
cultural memory, and commemoration pour out every year.[1]
Historian Kerwin L. Klein has observed, "Memory is replacing
old favorites—*nature, culture, language*—as the word most
commonly paired with history and that shift is remaking
historical imagination."[2] Perhaps the best of these recent
works is by the German scholar Jan Assmann, the famous
Egyptologist. To Assmann, the "past is not simply 'received'
by the present. The present is 'haunted' by the past and the
past is modeled, invented, reinvented, and reconstructed by
the present." In his groundbreaking study of how Moses and
Egypt were remembered in Western thought, Assmann dubs
this form of historical analysis "mnemohistory." He insists

that this line of investigation "is concerned not with the past as such, but only with the past as it is remembered."[3]

Native peoples consciously and subconsciously construct their own views of the past. That is their right, as it is with other peoples. I have become fascinated by this process, namely, how and why Native Americans develop certain views of the past, ones that sometimes make little sense to the academy of scholars or unfortunately bring academics and Indian communities into conflict.[4]

I am not the first historian to consider this particular subject. In interviewing 186 Sioux Indians at the Pine Ridge Reservation, historians Roy Rosenzweig and David Thelen learned that family was "the primary source of personal identity of locus of historical memory." From that, "more collective identities as members of a tribe, as residents of Pine Ridge, and as American Indians flowed." These Sioux shared a "set of historical references to particular events, places and people [e.g., Columbus's arrival in the Americas, treaties, the Wounded Knee Massacre of 1890, the armed occupation of Wounded Knee in 1973] that they repeatedly invoked and used, albeit not always in the same ways," which often were contrary to what they read in schoolbooks. To them, history also meant betrayal by whites; however, by recounting injustices, Rosenzweig and Thelen found, the Sioux were more motivated to preserve as much of the old ways—beadwork, language, traditions—as possible.[5]

For the past thirty-seven years, I had the privilege of researching and writing about the history of the Six Nations—the Mohawks, Oneidas, Onondagas, Cayugas, Senecas, and

Tuscaroras—as well as those other peoples, Iroquoian, Algonquian, and Siouan, absorbed into their famous confederacy. I have combined archival research with extensive fieldwork on many of the Iroquoian reservations and reserves in the United States and Canada. In working with the Oneida Nation of Indians of Wisconsin for nearly three decades, I have learned that collective memory of a people—namely, heritage—takes priority over anything that historians in the academy write about. To the Wisconsin Oneidas, history is lived memory, not the abstract version produced by scholars. Collective memory cannot easily be challenged since it takes on a quasiritualistic life of its own, as it deals with one's kin and one's Oneida identity.[6] Much like the Sioux of Rosenzweig and Thelen's study, the Wisconsin Oneidas see history in kinship terms and use it in conscious efforts to maintain and strengthen identity.

In the past, collective memory among the Iroquois, including the Oneidas, was reinforced by a most important ritual—the condolence council. This ancient rite led League chiefs to recount the past and the notable exploits of deceased honored leaders. It was a reminder to those being raised to chief of their responsibilities to their contemporary society. The ritual also taught the Indians and their guests, including white diplomats such as Sir William Johnson, about the long-standing achievements of the Iroquois League of Peace and Power and emphasized the relevance of the past to the present.[7]

The Oneidas' collective memory, their heritage, is shaped by stories, some true and others not, told and repeated, especially about the time period from the American Revolution through the Civil War. Historian John R. Gillis has observed, "Memories help us make sense of the world we live in; and memory work is, like any other kind of physical or mental labor, embedded in complex class, gender, and power relations that determine what is remembered (or forgotten), by whom, and for what end."[8] Gillis's statement is true for all peoples, including the Oneida Indians living at Oneida, New York; Oneida, Wisconsin; and Southwold, Ontario.

Although there is the propensity of accepting the insiders' view of their own history, some of these Oneida stories are not completely true or even verifiable, but that in itself does not make these heritage stories unimportant to scholars. The eminent historian of the African American experience and the Civil War, David Blight, has perceptively written:

> The historical memory of a people, a nation, or any aggregate evolves over time in relation to present needs and ever-changing contexts. Societies and the groups within them remember and use history as a source of coherence and identity, as a means of contending for power or place, and as a means of controlling access to whatever becomes normative in society. For better and worse, social memories—ceaselessly constructed versions of a group past—are the roots of identity formation. In spite of all we would like to think we have learned about how culture is invented and how heritage is a social construct that ultimately defines fixed definition, people jealously seek to own their pasts.[9]

Perhaps more than most, the Oneidas fit Blight's paradigm. All peoples, consciously and unconsciously, selectively draw from their past to meet the needs of the present. Today, much of the Oneidas' contemporary identity as a people, their collective memory, is based on their long military service as allies of the United States.[10]

Three Oneida stories illustrate how these extraordinary peoples construct their tribal heritage out of both facts and false assumptions:

    1. The Oneidas brought corn to General George Washington's army at Valley Forge. Certain Oneidas—men and at least one woman on the patriot side—were rewarded for service in the American Revolution by being given land by General Washington and a shawl by Martha Washington.

    2. The Oneidas defeated the British navy in the War of 1812.

    3. An Oneida—Private Cornelius Doxtator—under heavy fire helped rescue the body of General James Birdseye McPherson during the Atlanta Campaign in 1864, but he never received the Congressional Medal of Honor that he deserved.

Analyzing the accuracy and overall significance of these stories is in no way meant to demean the Oneidas and their oral traditions but to explain how these stories—true, partially true, or false—help define Oneida national identity. These three stories are quite distinct from other older ones passed down by Oneida elders, the most important one involving a great stone. Oneida Indians refer to themselves as OnCyoyaʔa·ká, "the People of the Standing Stone." According to Oneida beliefs, a granite boulder unlike any other found in central New York State suddenly appeared at their village near Oneida Lake. Whenever they moved within the vicinity, the stone, unaided by any human hands, followed them, appearing every time. Finally, when Oneida Castle was established, it remained there. Around this sacred stone, Oneidas conducted their great councils, where they resolved questions presented to them and worshipped the Creator. The missionary Jeremy Belknap, writing in 1796, stated that the followers of the Great Binding Law of the Iroquois, the non-Christian Oneidas, saw the stone as an "image of the deity" that was to be worshipped. Other commentators viewed the sacred stone as a great altar at which Oneidas prayed. In 1850 what was believed to be the Oneidas' sacred stone was dragged off by prominent citizens of central New York and placed in Forest Hill Cemetery just outside Utica; nevertheless, all Oneidas, including those in Wisconsin, despite this white cultural appropriation of the stone, still see the stone as the symbol of the continuity and survivability of the Oneida Nation. Today a replica is in front of the Radisson Hotel on Oneida lands near Green Bay, Wisconsin.[11]

The Oneida story of their participation on the American side during the Revolutionary War is intriguing and is the most widely repeated of the three stories of war. Oneidas still talk about General Marquis de Lafayette, how they won the Battle of Oriskany, and their suffering as refugees of war at Schenectady. To this day, Wisconsin Oneidas hold their powwow on July 4 each year.[12]

Although some Oneidas splintered off and joined the sizable contingent of the Six Nations on the British side during the American Revolution, the vast majority of Oneidas, encouraged by their pro-American missionary Samuel Kirkland, faithfully served George Washington's rebel army (as did the Oneidas' allies the Tuscaroras). Eleven Oneidas served as officers in the American army, and, to this day, Oneida folklore is filled with references to their service in the patriots' quest for independence. Among the Oneida heroes of the Revolution are Peter Bread, Blatcop, Henry Cornelius (later the founder of the Handsome Lake religion among the Oneidas), Hanyost, Paul Powless, and Thawengarakwen (Honyery Doxtator). At Oriskany, Blatcop, one of the Oneida warriors there, under intense British fire heroically charged the enemy three times during this major battle of the Saratoga campaign, while Dolly Cobus, Honyery Doxtator's wife, took her husband's place in the battle after he had been wounded in the right wrist. Hanyost distinguished himself at the siege of Fort Stanwix as a lieutenant under General Peter Gansevoort's overall command. Moreover, Oneida chiefs Skenandoah and Good Peter, despite their advanced ages at the time, faithfully served the Americans as messengers from General Philip Schuyler, only to be arrested and harshly confined as prisoners of war by the British in 1780.[13]

Unfortunately, despite the grand nature of the story, there is no evidence that Oneidas brought bushels of corn to feed Washington's army during the worst days at Valley Forge. Yet, as Jack Campisi has written, this is "a well and favorably accepted" fact, even though "it is not a tradition held strongly by those Oneidas who left New York and moved to Canada (the Oneida Reserve of the Oneidas of the Thames) in the 1840s." Campisi adds, "Support for the rebel cause sixty-five years earlier did not sit well with the Oneidas' new hosts [British Canada]."[14]

Related to the first story are items allegedly given to the Oneidas for their service in the American Revolution. Oneidas in New York and Wisconsin told me of a shawl, hat, and bonnet given to them by General Washington for their help at Valley Forge. According to various versions of this story, the shawl was presented to Polly Cooper by Washington, by his wife, Martha, or by Benjamin Franklin in recognition of the tribe's service in bringing corn to the Continental Army at Valley Forge. Cooper allegedly refused payment after teaching the grateful Americans how to prepare the corn.[15] I could not verify this story in the documentary record, although I found records in the New York State Archives to one Polly Cooper, a thirty-one-year-old Oneida woman receiving a pension for service in the War of 1812. This Polly Cooper would have been too young—she would have been born around 1782—to have been the same Oneida woman of the American Revolutionary period.[16]

One verifiable Oneida story told to me in Wisconsin involves Honyery (Hanyerry) Doxtator (Thawengarakwen) and Hanyost, two of the Indian officers in the patriot army, who were given land after the war by General Washington as a reward for their valuable military service.[17] Oneidas today claim that Honyery's wife, Dolly Cobus, the so-called Indian Molly Pitcher, was also presented with a gift of lands for her heroic deeds during the war.[18] One Oneida matron indicated that the land ceded to the Oneidas was somewhere near Red Hook. I quickly but inaccurately assumed that she was confused. Growing up in the "Middle Kingdom" known as Brooklyn, where there is a Red Hook, I could not imagine General Washington—then or now—giving this section of my "'hood" to the Indians. I then came to a second inaccurate conclusion, namely, that the elderly Oneida woman was referring to Red Hook, Dutchess County, New York, the exact place where a prominent Oneida family, the Chrisjohns, whom she knew well, formerly resided. Yet, I was also well aware that the Chrisjohns had come into the area only in the 1950s, and besides, Dutchess County was not part of the New Military Tract set up as bounty lands for veterans of the American Revolution.

In time, I was able to pinpoint the exact location of lands that the Oneida elder had meant. Oneidas, including Washington's Oneida officers Hanyost and Honyere, had been granted military bounty lands in the town of Junius, totaling three thousand acres, in 1791. Not too far away, in Wolcott, New York, is Red Springs. These lands, taken from the Cayugas during the American Revolution, became part of the New Military Tract. Perhaps wary of settling on the lands of other Iroquois such as the vanquished Cayugas, the Oneidas chose to sell their lots on May 26, 1809, for $23,000. Although the Oneida elder was not quite right about the details, my assumptions about her memory were incorrect. I was, however, unable to confirm or discount the story of Dolly Cobus receiving lands.[19]

Taken at face value, the story that the Oneidas tell about their role in the War of 1812 is the least believable tale of the three. Nevertheless, this incredible story of defeating the mighty British navy is nearly 100 percent accurate. As early as 1852, the Oneidas were retelling this story in a determined effort to seek federal monetary compensation for their service at the Battle of Sandy Creek.[20]

In May of 1814, a military detachment of over 120 irregulars, mostly Oneidas but including a sprinkling of Brothertown, Onondaga, and Stockbridge Indians, made their way through the rough terrain north of Oneida Lake, unaware that their forced march would lead to a dramatic American victory at Sandy Creek. The expedition then shifted westward, reaching the American fort at Oswego, where they were supplied with cartridges for their rifles, firewood, scissors, and U.S. Army–issued rations and were outfitted with blankets, vermilion cloth, shirts, and two pairs of shoes for each man. This contingent was soon sent to serve as a shoreline escort for an American supply convoy of bateaux heading for Sackets Harbor. Armed with their own hunting rifles brought from their homes, these Indians going off to battle had long heard elders recount stories of their military exploits, their warriors' heroism at the Battle of Oriskany in the summer of 1777, their loyal commitment to General Washington, and their admiration for the Marquis de Lafayette, who helped recruit them for military service in the American Revolution. Around council fires, they had listened to Oneida veterans talk about the greatness of Blatcop, Peter Bread, Hanyerry, Hanyost, Two Kettles Together, and the boy warrior Peter Powless, all famous Oneidas who had fought on the patriot side in the War of Brothers that raged from 1775 to 1783. Attempting to replicate that warrior experience, Oneidas enlisted in President James Madison's army in 1813.[21]

The Oneidas, including some of the most prominent tribesmen of the era—Peter Elm, Daniel Bread, Henry Cornelius, and Adam Skenandoah—were a vital part of the overall defense of Sackets Harbor, the only American-held ship launching center on Lake Ontario during most of the War of 1812. The port was slowly being strangled by an effective British blockade. In the dead of night, on the evening of May 28 and into the early morning hours of May 29, American Master-Commandant Melancthon Woolsey attempted to break the blockade by sneaking nineteen bateaux transporting naval guns and heavy cable past the British naval force.

The American supply fleet pulled into Sandy Creek to await an escort of troops being dispatched from Sackets Harbor. British Commander Stephen Popham learned of the attempt to resupply Sackets Harbor and dispatched a force of three gunboats, four smaller craft, and nearly two hundred sailors and marines to thwart the Americans.[22]

The British contingent soon spotted the masts of the American bateaux, which had now sailed up some distance into Sandy Creek away from its entrance on Lake Ontario. Unaware that the American supply vessels were protected by numerous American-allied Indian riflemen hidden on the banks of the creek, Popham, going against orders, directed his force to pursue the American bateaux into Sandy Creek. The British navy was soon ambushed by these Indians coming from the south and by other American marines, dragoons, and riflemen on the north shore of the creek coming from Sackets Harbor.[23]

The British forces were cut to pieces in the ensuing firefight, known as the Battle of Big Sandy or the Battle of Sandy Creek. Fourteen British sailors were killed, and twenty-eight were wounded. Popham's three gunboats, which contained Congreve rockets, were captured by American forces. Subsequently, the much-needed American supply bateaux reached Sackets Harbor. The heavy cable and naval guns were then used to help outfit the USS *Superior,* a sixty-two-gun warship, which was launched and which weakened the British control of Lake Ontario. To this day, Oneidas have an oral tradition of this momentous battle, the day they defeated the mighty British navy and changed the course of the War of 1812.[24]

The third story, largely handed down by descendants of one prominent family, involves Cornelius Doxtator, a well-respected Oneida of the mid-nineteenth century, and his role as a private in Company F, Fourteenth Wisconsin Volunteer Infantry, a unit that included thirty-eight other Oneida Indians during the American Civil War.[25] Doxtator later claimed in his Civil War pension application that, under enemy fire, he rescued the body of General James Birdseye McPherson, the highest ranking Union general killed in action in the Civil War, near Peachtree Creek, on July 22, 1864, during the Atlanta campaign.[26] Instead of being awarded the Congressional Medal of Honor for his efforts, he was given a furlough to return home to Oneida. When he went home, he contracted smallpox, was too sick to return to his regiment, and was subsequently listed as a deserter.[27]

Doxtator's extraordinary claim can be disputed in several ways. The soldier never mentioned the rescue and gave an alternate explanation for his furlough:

> About 15 Indians in my Co. and regiment. I was the only one who could speak English and almost everything had to be done through me as interpreter. We got to Atlanta and I understood that we were to remain there a month. I had heard from my family that they were sick and destitute. I had not received any pay yet and I went to General [Francis Preston] Blair and told him and he gave me a furlough of 30 days. I had only been home about 8 days when I was taken sick with small pox. I had been in the service about 8 months when I got furloughed.[28]

Moreover, at the time of McPherson's death, F Company Indians were pinned down by Confederate fire. On the afternoon of July 22, the Fourteenth Wisconsin were engaged in repulsing a Confederate advance in the Battle of Bald Hill. They had been on picket duty when the Confederates attacked. They, along with Companies E and F and the Eleventh Iowa Volunteer Infantry, dug in, holding "the small fort on the hill and the immediate line of works connected with it." Lieutenant Colonel J. C. Abercrombie of the Eleventh Iowa later wrote in his official report: "Many acts of bravery were performed by officers and men of the regiment which might be mentioned did time and opportunity permit."[29]

Other evidence suggests that Private Doxtator was not involved in the rescue of McPherson's body. Three of Cornelius Doxtator's comrades-in-arms in Company F—Henry Coulon, George S. Doxtator, and Henry Stephens—dictated affidavits to the U.S. Bureau of Pensions in support of their fellow Oneida's pension increase application. Not one of them mentioned the private's rescue of McPherson's body, a fact that would have been worthy of description. Instead, they described Doxtator's run-in with a stick and his injury to his "private parts."[30] These statements were repeated by the private's neighbors at Oneida and by his physician who had tended to his medical needs for thirty-five years. Equally revealing, there are no letters from his sons, George and Paul, his comrades in the regiment, in the pension records to confirm this important event.

Perhaps the embarrassment of being injured in this manner at a time when his Oneida comrades were dying on the battlefield led him to concoct this story. Is this a proper assumption of what transpired? Did Private Doxtator lie about his military record? Although this could easily be inferred, I cannot conclude that he did. After the incident, Doxator participated in the momentous siege of Atlanta, the decisive Union victory that signaled the beginning of the end of the Confederate States of America. After reporting for duty in August through mid-October during those momentous days of the war, he is listed as a deserter from November 1864 onward.[31] It should be pointed out that the word "desertion" was used for soldiers who were AWOL (absent without leave) during the Civil War. The U.S. Bureau of Pensions accepted Doxtator's affidavits that he had been given official furlough to return home in the fall of 1864 and that, while home, he had contracted smallpox, which delayed his return to his unit until he was officially mustered out with a general discharge in May, 1865.[32] There is also evidence that while recuperating, Doxtator remained loyal to the Union cause. He later claimed that he went to Madison after he recovered from smallpox but was rejected because of poor health. There is also evidence that he helped in recruiting Oneida soldiers for the war effort while back on the reservation during his convalescence.[33]

I believe that there are several explanations for Doxtator's story. This unfortunate Oneida clearly suffered for decades as a result of his Civil War service. Historian Eric T. Dean has written about the aftermath of the conflict, suggesting that veterans suffered from the high rates of what today we call post-traumatic stress disorder.[34] Doxtator's military records, especially affidavits found in his pension record, confirm much but not all of the Oneida soldier's story. More important, they poignantly reveal the torment that Private Doxtator faced during and after the Civil War. Besides having to counter the false charge of desertion, his health rapidly deteriorated. By the early 1890s, he had had smallpox, had a "continuous pain in the head above the eyebrows," had limited vision, was going deaf, had severe rheumatism, gasped for breath, was affected by a myriad of respiratory problems, suffered from a hernia with a perforation the size of "a small orange," and showed the initial signs of dementia. He could do no manual labor and was totally dependent on his Oneida neighbors and relatives.[35]

Indeed, the death of McPherson was a defining moment in the entire Atlanta Campaign, one that became indelible in Private Doxtator's mind, which was failing by the mid-1880s. The general's death became his touchstone, his badge of honor for serving in the Grand Army of the West. To Americans of the postwar generation, McPherson and his heroic death took on legendary proportions. To include oneself in the legend would give more meaning to one's postwar existence, a miserable one at that, filled with chronic illnesses and extreme poverty. Yet, as a survivor of the war, Private Doxtator was undoubtedly affected by embarrassment describing how and where he was injured, the same day his fellow Oneida Simon King had paid the ultimate sacrifice. Consequently, I would rather believe that Doxtator was a casualty of war, that he suffered from post-traumatic stress disorder, than conclude that he fabricated the story for profit and fame. The reasons are very clear to me. The U.S. Bureau of Pensions awarded him a pension and the affidavits and other supporting evidence verified everything that Private Doxtator claimed except the McPherson story. He was described in the records as an upstanding, moral man by his Oneida comrades and neighbors, his white doctor, and his white attorney. As a survivor of the hell known as the Civil War, he continued to bear the physical and psychological scars of the conflict for nearly a half century until his death in 1911.[36]

The Oneidas' collective memories about their significant involvement on the side of the Americans in 1776, 1812, and 1861 today serve as a vital role in maintaining identity. They have much to be proud of concerning their roles; however, remembering their military service in the past serves a key function in the present. As Assmann has observed, "Events tend to be forgotten unless they live on in collective memory." He adds, "There is no meaning in history unless these distinctions are remembered. The reason for this living on, lies in the continuous relevance of these events."[37]

All of these stories emphasize the Oneidas' heroic sacrifice on behalf of the United States. In the American Revolution, the Oneidas lost many lives, and their main village was destroyed by Joseph Brant and his Mohawk warriors. The Oneidas' loyalty to the American cause led them to impoverishment as refugees at Schenectady in the last years of the war. The decision of most of the Oneidas to support the Americans undermined their role in the councils of the Iroquois since the majority of the Six Nations served the British or attempted to remain neutral during the American Revolution. Even to this day, the Oneidas are looked at askance by some of the chiefs at Onondaga for the decisions they made in the American Revolution in support of the patriot cause. At the federal Fort Stanwix Treaty of 1784, they and the Tuscaroras were treated by the United States as allies, not as conquered nations as were the other four nations of the Iroquois. In November 1794, although the Oneidas were signatories at the Treaty with the Six Nations at Canandaigua, the United States also treated with the Oneidas separately the next month. Although they were dispossessed of over five million acres of their tribal estate in so-called state treaties in 1785 at Fort Herkimer and in 1788 at Fort Schuyler and lost substantial acreage to the state from 1795 to 1809, the Oneidas nevertheless enlisted in the U.S. Army in 1813, hoping that their Great Father in Washington would finally carry out his past treaty commitments of friendship and protection.[38]

It is this latter point that you still hear in Oneida homes as well as tribal circles today, namely, that they have an obligation to serve, and that the outside—Washington and especially Albany—need to reciprocate because of their sacrifice. Family military service is ingrained, and children and grandchildren follow the footsteps of their elders, much like the military tradition in parts of the U.S. South today; however, there is more to it than that. The chain of friendship established by Chiefs Good Peter, Skenandoah, and others during the American Revolutionary era still helps define Oneida identity. From Oriskany to Baghdad, they have served, in part to remind Americans that they have an obligation to fulfill their part of the alliance made in 1777.

Although they periodically remind outsiders of their impressive military service throughout American history, Oneidas mostly stress their role in the War of Independence on the side of George Washington and the patriot cause. During their July 4 festivities throughout the nineteenth century, chiefs, in the manner of the traditional condolence council ritual, addressed a gathering of tribal members and non-Indian guests to their Wisconsin reservation telling of the great Oneida leaders of the past and their heroic exploits at

Oriskany or Valley Forge. In a conscious effort to generate good will in their new location in Wisconsin, they showed their non-Indian guests that they were loyal Americans worthy of respect.[39]

With pressures for removal from Wisconsin building before the Civil War, chiefs such as Daniel Bread fully understood the importance of cooperation with the white world in an effort to fight off local, state, and federal efforts at tribal dispossession. In typical fashion, Bread, on July 4, 1854, insisted that "the Oneidas, ever friendly towards your fathers [founding fathers], could not be alienated from them either by the threats or persuasions of their foes." He stated that his people's commitment to General Washington led the Oneidas to paint "their tomahawks red in blood of the enemies of your people." Chief Bread pointed out his people's sacrifice: "Many of their best warriors were slain, but their own children knew not the resting place of their bodies." Sadly, he added, "There are no monuments erected to show where they fell." Reaffirming Oneida loyalty to "our Great Father," Bread asked that in return Washington would protect them "whenever we are in danger of trouble."[40]

Wisconsin Oneidas continued to use the stories of the American Revolution well into the twentieth century.[41] In attempting to fight off the conversion of trust lands to fee simple patents subject to taxation and foreclosure after the Burke Act of 1906, Oneidas once again brought up the stories of the American Revolution and made reference to Oneida military service and loyalty to the United States. In a letter of July 23, 1918, addressed to President Wilson, Paul Doxtator, Cornelius Doxtator's son, pointed out that his family members had fought on the American side from

Bunker Hill onward and were killed in action fighting the British in the War of 1812, that he and his brother George and his father had served in the Civil War, and that his son John was now part of the American Expeditionary Force fighting Germans in Europe.[42]

Anthropologist Anthony W. Wonderley has written that the Oneidas "dusted off" the stories of the American Revolution after *United States v. Boylan* (1920), a case in which Oneidas successfully fought to save their remaining reservation lands in New York. By the late 1920s and after, these Oneida stories began to reappear in central New York newspapers just when the Oneida modern land claims movement began to gain momentum.[43] Hence, Oneida loyal service to the United States stood in direct contrast to the federal and state goverments' failure to carry out their responsibilities to these patriotic Indians. By the 1960s and 1970s, the Oneidas renewed efforts in pushing their claim, almost always making reference to their extensive military contributions, especially their remarkable service in the American Revolution.[44]

The stories told by Oneidas, whether accurate, half-accurate, or fiction, tell more than simply an Oneida perspective of history. They also reflect cultural values and aspirations. Although Oneidas want to still remain culturally distinct, they also have a desire to be recognized and included in the larger sweep of American history. Unlike the Oneida story of the Standing Stone, the three stories discussed are inclusive, rather than distinctive, in their focus. They are saying to us that we were there with you at the darkest days of your history—at the Saratoga Campaign of 1777, the British blockade of Lake Ontario in 1813–14, and the siege of Atlanta in the summer of 1864. Whether false assumptions or not, the Oneidas have purposefully constructed these stories, holding on to them for generations as a reminder that they too were and are important and have had extraordinary leaders; however, there is much more to it. Instead of ancient condolence council ceremonies that formerly acted to reinforce their feelings about the greatness of the past and reminded both Oneidas and their guests of their mutual obligations to one another, Oneidas now use these stories as cultural touchstones to reinforce their heritage, their collective memory, their national identity, one that is not entirely exclusive from the American national identity.

Today, the Wisconsin Oneidas use the past in a variety of ways. They sponsor annual history conferences that more aptly should be deemed heritage events. Participants include numerous community peoples and a few trusted scholars. The Wisconsin Oneidas also maintain an elaborate cultural heritage department and publish a newsletter with its version of these Indians' past, articles that have included aspects of Oneida and Iroquoian cultural and religious traditions, the effects of the Dawes General Allotment Act, and accounts of famous Oneida leaders in history. The Oneida Cultural Heritage Department also houses the voluminous stories collected by Oneida elders from 1938 to 1942 under the auspices of the Works Progress Administration. This Oneida Language and Folklore Project, administered by anthropologists Morris Swadesh, Floyd Lounsbury, and Harry Basehart, is a remarkable oral history collection on every aspect of Oneida life from the time of these New York Indians' arrival in Wisconsin, then Michigan Territory, in the 1820s.[45] Working under contract from the nation, L. Gordon McLester

III, an Oneida public historian who also runs the Oneida history conferences and who is the founder of the Oneida Historical Society, has conducted more than three hundred videotaped interviews with elders about events, festivities, peoples, places, and traditions. Both the WPA Oneida Language and Folklore Project and the collection of recent videotaped interviews are slowly becoming the sacred texts of present-day Oneida life, used by the community to reinforce a collective sense of identity. In many ways, they are more important to the people's sense of their past than monographs written by Jack Campisi, William N. Fenton, Barbara Graymont, Laurence M. Hauptman, Francis Jennings, or Elisabeth Tooker.

Historian Eric Foner has observed that "versions of the past provide the raw materials for nationalist ideologies and patriotic sentiments." Foner adds that all peoples, unintentionally or otherwise, construct the story of the past "in response to new information, new methodologies, and new political, social, and cultural imperatives."[46] Native peoples, including the Wisconsin Oneidas, are no exception to this rule.

Notes

I would like to thank L. Gordon McLester III for his continuing help in understanding the history of his Oneida people.

1. The scholarly literature on the subject of memory is too immense to cite in its entirety. The following have significantly affected my own thinking: Jan Assmann, *Moses the Egyptian: The Memory of Egypt in Western Thought* (Cambridge: Harvard University Press, 1997); Yosef Hayim Yerushalmi, *Zakhor: Jewish History and Jewish*

Memory, revised ed. (New York: Schocken Books, 1989); David W. Blight, "A Quarrel Forgotten or a Revolution Remembered? Reunion and Race in the Memory of the Civil War, 1875–1913," in *Beyond the Battlefield: Race, Memory, and the American Civil War,* ed. David W. Blight (Amherst: University of Massachusetts Press, 2002), 120; Paul Connerton, *How Societies Remember* (Cambridge: Cambridge University Press, 1989); Thomas Butler, ed., *Memory: History, Culture, and the Mind* (Oxford: Basil Blackwell, 1989); Eric Hobsbawm and Terence Ranger, eds., *The Invention of Tradition* (Cambridge: Cambridge University Press, 1983); Michael Kammen, *Mystic Chords of Memory: The Transformation of Tradition in American Culture* (New York: Alfred A. Knopf, 1991); and John Bodnar, *Remaking America: Public Memory, Commemoration, and Patriotism in the Twentieth Century* (Princeton, N.J.: Princeton University Press, 1992). For an analysis of how one present-day Native American community (the Oglala Sioux of the Pine Ridge Reservation) remembers and uses the past, see Roy Rosenzweig and David Thelen, *The Presence of the Past: Popular Uses of History in American Life* (New York: Columbia University Press, 1998), 147–76. I should like to thank my colleague David Krikun, associate professor of history emeritus at SUNY New Paltz, for bringing much of the rich literature on memory to my attention.

2. Kerwin L. Klein, "On the Emergence of Memory in Historical Discourse," *Representations* 69 (Winter 2000): 128. I have also found especially insightful Richard J. Bernstein's review essay on Avishai Margalit's *The Ethics of Memory* (2002): "The Culture of Memory," *History and Theory* 43 (December 2004): 165–78.

3. Assmann, *Moses the Egyptian,* 9–10.

4. See Laurence M. Hauptman, *Tribes and Tribulations: Misconceptions about American Indians and Their Histories* (Albuquerque: University of New Mexico Press, 1995), 27–38.

5. Rosenzweig and Thelen, *Presence of the Past,* 162–76.

6. Yosef Hayim Yerushalmi has brilliantly written that Jewish memory was preserved by the priests and holy people, not by "a nation of historians," and that memory "flowed above all, through two channels: ritual and recital." The ritualistic nature of the Iroquoian world and its emphasis on oral traditions seem very similar. Yerushalmi, *Zakhor,* 10–11.

7. For the best treatment of the Iroquois condolence council, see William N. Fenton, *The Great Law and the Longhouse: A Political History of the Iroquois Confederacy* (Norman: University of Oklahoma Press, 1998), 3–18, 135–42. For its importance in Iroquoian diplomacy, see William N. Fenton, "Structure, Continuity, and Change in the Process of Iroquois Treaty-Making," in *The History and Culture of Iroquois Diplomacy: An Interdisciplinary Guide to the Treaties of the Six Nations and Their League,* ed. Francis Jennings et al. (Syracuse, N.Y.: Syracuse University Press, 1985), 3–36. For the council's legacy among the Oneidas, see Laurence M. Hauptman and L. Gordon McLester III, *Chief Daniel Bread and the Oneida Nation of Indians of Wisconsin* (Norman: University of Oklahoma Press, 2002), 122–25.

8. John R. Gillis, "Memory and Identity: The History of a Relationship," in *Commemorations: The Politics of National Identity,* ed. John R. Gillis (Princeton, N.J.: Princeton University Press, 1994), 3. Today, three Oneida communities—Oneida, Wisconsin; Southwold, Ontario; and Oneida, New York—are tied by Iroquoian culture, kinship, and similar historical experiences before 1838. A fourth Oneida community exists at the Six Nations Reserve at Ohsweken, Ontario. This fourth community is comprised largely of Oneidas descended from those who followed Mohawk Joseph Brant and joined the British in the American Revolution, going into Canada after the war. They have fewer political ties to the other three major Oneida communities since these three communities are descended largely from the majority of Oneidas who joined the American army in the American Revolution.

9. Blight, "Quarrel Forgotten," 120.

10. Political scientist Tom Holm, a Cherokee-Creek veteran of Vietnam, has written about American Indian service in the U.S. armed forces: "Native American veterans identify themselves with a community (tribe) and with that community's specific traditions." Holm adds, "Their sense of peoplehood is directly linked to place (homeland/holy land) and a shared sacred history. They tend to think of themselves as warriors of an older, sacred tradition, but placed in a changed set of circumstances." Qtd. in Matthew Dennis, *Red, White, and Blue Letter Days* (Ithaca, N.Y.: Cornell University Press, 2002), 67.

11. A. D. Gridley, *History of the Town of Kirkland* (New York: Hurd and Houghton, 1874), 7–8; Jeremy Belknap, *Journal of a Tour from Boston to Oneida, June 1796,* ed. George Dexter (Cambridge, Mass.: John Wilson, 1882), 21–24; Timothy Dwight, *Travels in New England and New York,* 1822, ed. Barbara Miller Solomon (Cambridge: Belknap Press of Harvard University, 1969), 149. For a fascinating analysis of the Oneida Standing Stone and its importance to both the Oneida Indians and non-Indians of central New York, see Anthony W. Wonderley, *Oneida Iroquois Folklore, Myth, and History: New York Oral Narrative from the Notes of H. E. Allen and Others* (Syracuse, N.Y.: Syracuse University Press, 2004), 1–4, 24–31.

12. Historian Matthew Dennis has observed that Independence Day has flourished in American Indian communities "because the holiday was foisted on Indians and because the fete offered them opportunities to preserve traditions or invent ways to survive." Dennis, *Red, White, and Blue,* 67. In the case of the Oneidas, Dennis's latter point is accurate, but I do not see July 4 as being foisted on them. See Hauptman and McLester, *Chief Daniel Bread,* 117–26.

13. See, e.g., the stories recounted by Gloria Halbritter, Loretta Metoxen, et al. in "Oneida Traditions," in *The Oneida Indian Experience: Two Perspectives,* ed. Laurence M. Hauptman and Jack Campisi

(Syracuse, N.Y.: Syracuse University Press, 1988), 145–46. For Oneida history during the American Revolution, see Barbara Graymont, "The Oneidas in the American Revolution," in Hauptman and Campesi, *Oneida Indian Experience,* 31–42; Barbara Graymont, *The Iroquois in the American Revolution* (Syracuse, N.Y.: Syracuse University Press, 1972), 132–41; Karim M. Tiro, "The People of the Standing Stone: The Oneida Indian Nation from Revolution Through Removal, 1765–1840" (PhD diss., University of Pennsylvania, Philadelphia, 1999), 99–146; and Joseph T. Glatthaar and James Kirby Martin, *Forgotten Allies: The Oneida Indians and the American Revolution* (New York: Hill and Wang, 2006).

14. Jack Campisi, "Inventing Indian Traditions," unpublished manuscript in author's possession; Glatthaar and Martin, *Forgotten Allies,* 205.

15. Halbritter, Metoxen, et al., "Oneida Traditions," 144–45. For more on this story, see Tiro, "People of the Standing Stone," 99–100; Glatthaar and Martin, *Forgotten Allies,* 208.

16. Abstract of Pension Application No. 10006, Records of the New York State Adjutant General's Office, Claims, Applications and Awards for Service in the War of 1812, Division of Military and Naval Affairs, New York State Archives, Albany.

17. Laurence M. Hauptman, Oneida (Wisconsin) field notes, 1978 (in author's possession).

18. Halbritter, Metoxen, et al., "Oneida Traditions," 146.

19. *The Balloting Book and Other Documents Relating to Military Bounty Lands in the State of New York* (Albany, N.Y.: Packard and Van Benthuysen, 1825), 140, 180 (town of Junius "awards" of Cayuga lands to Oneidas for military service). Apparently, they or their heirs sold these military bounty lands, a total of eight lots totaling three thousand acres, on May 26, 1809, for $23,000. L. P. Gillett Deed, New York Surveyor-General's Land Papers, ser. 2, A40167, Box 12, folders 81B, 83B, 94A, New York State Archives, Albany.

20. See U.S. Congress, Senate, Committee of Claims, *Report Regarding Compensation for the Capture of Three Gun Boats* [in the War of 1812—petition of Oneida Indians], 32nd Cong., 1st sess., Senate Report 286, July 6, 1852, Serial Set 631. See also A. D. Bonesteel to A. B. Greenwood (commissioner of Indian Affairs), July 8, 1859, OIA, M234, National Archives (hereafter NA), Record Group (hereafter RG) 75, Records of the Green Bay Agency, Microfilm Reel 323.

21. The treatment of the Battle of Big Sandy (Sandy Creek) is derived from the following: J. Mackay Hitsman, *The Incredible War of 1812: A Military History* (Toronto: University of Toronto Press, 1998), 155, 172; Douglas R. Hickey, *The War of 1812: A Forgotten Conflict* (Urbana: University of Illinois Press, 1989), 185; Greg Chester, *The Battle of Big Sandy* (Adams, N.Y.: Historical Association of South Jefferson County, 1981).

22. U.S. Congress, Senate, Committee of Claims, *Report Regarding Compensation.*

23. Ibid.

24. Ibid.

25. Laurence M. Hauptman, *The Iroquois in the Civil War: From Battlefield to Reservation* (Syracuse, N.Y.: Syracuse University Press, 1993), 67–83.

26. For General McPherson, see Albert Castel, *Decision in the West: The Atlanta Campaign of 1864* (Lawrence: University Press of Kansas, 1992), 79–81, 265–66, 411.

27. This story was told to me by various Wisconsin Oneidas on at least five separate occasions over the past twenty-five years. Hauptman, field notes, 1978–2003. Affidavit of Cornelius Doxtator, August 1885; Cornelius Doxtator's Original Pension Claim, November 29, 1887, Cornelius Doxtator's Civil War Pension Record (hereafter CWPR), Certificate No. 852,104, Records of the U.S. War Department, NA, RG 94; Cornelius Doxtator's Completed Military Service

Record, F Company, 14th Wisconsin Volunteer Infantry, NA, RG 94, Records of the Adjutant General's Office.

28. Cornelius Doxtator, Original Pension Claim, December 16, 1885, Cornelius Doxtator's CWPR.

29. U.S. War Department, *The War of the Rebellion: A Compilation of the Official Recoords of the Union and Confederate Armies,* 128 vols. (Washington, D.C.: Government Printing Office, 1880–1901), ser. 1, vol. 38, part 111: 599–600.

30. Henry Coulon, George S. Doxtator, and Henry Stephens, Oneidas in Company F, confirmed the accident: Affidavit of Henry Stephens, July 21, 1888; Affidavits of George S. Doxtator, August 11, 19, 1891, August 19, 1899; Affidavits of Henry Coulon, September 12, 1891, June 15, 1893; Affidavit of Henry Coulon and George S. Doxtator, April 12, 1905; Cornelius Doxtator CWPR.

31. "The charge of desertion removed. He was absent without leave from Oct. 22, 1864 to April 20, 1865." R. C. Drum (U.S. adjutant general) to Commissioner of Pensions, June 12, 1889, Cornelius Doxtator CWPR.

32. Cornelius Doxtator's Compiled Military Service Record, NA, RG 94; F Company, 14th Wisconsin Blue and Red Regimental Books, Wisconsin Historical Society, Madison.

33. Affidavit of Cornelius Doxtator, August 1885 (stamped August 20, 1885); Cornelius Doxtator's Original Claim for a Pension, December 16, 1885; Affidavit of Cornelius Doxtator's Affidavit, January 25, 1888, Cornelius Doxtator's CWPR. Deborah B. Martin, in her history of Brown County, quotes Provost Marshal E. C. Merrill of Wisconsin: "The Oneida Indians, always a warlike people, organized a company of sharpshooters under command of Cornelius Doxtator." Besides reinforcing stereotypes about the Oneidas, either Martin or Merrill misidentified Doxtator as being in the Third Wisconsin. I believe that this was the same Cornelius Doxtator of Company F,

Fourteenth Wisconsin, which would confirm at least part of his story. Deborah B. Martin, *History of Brown County, Wisconsin: Past and Present,* 2 vols. (Chicago, Ill.: S. J. Clarke, 1913), 1:209.

34. Eric T. Dean, Jr., *Shook over Hell: Post-Traumatic Stress, Vietnam and the Civil War* (Cambridge: Harvard University Press, 1997), 46–69.

35. Cornelius Doxtator's Original Claim for a Pension, December 16, 1885; Doxtator's Claim for Invalid Pension, February 25, 1890; Doxtator's Affidavits of January 25, August 11, 1888, September 17, 1890, March 2, 1892; Doxtator's Invalid Pension Application, May 4, 1889, April 3, 1901; Bureau of Pensions Surgeon's Certificate, April 3, 1901; Affidavit of Dr. Israel Green (Doxtator's Green Bay physician), September 14, 1885; Acting Commissioner Bureau of Pensions to Edward Doxtator, July 24, 1907, Cornelius Doxtator CWPR.

36. For more on the suffering of veterans, see Dean, *Shook over Hell,* 46–69.

37. Assmann, *Moses the Egyptian,* 9–10.

38. See U.S. Congress, Senate, Committee of Claims, *Report Regarding Compensation,* and Laurence M. Hauptman, *Conspiracy of Interests: Iroquois Dispossession and the Rise of New York State* (Syracuse, N.Y.: Syracuse University Press, 1999), chapters 1–6.

39. Hauptman and McLester, *Chief Daniel Bread,* 121–26.

40. *Green Bay Advocate,* July 4, 1854.

41. From 1928 to 1950 J. H. Wenberg, the Methodist missionary to the Wisconsin Oneidas, collected numerous stories of these Indians' roles in the American Revolution. "Notes on the Early History of the Oneidas and of the Iroquois Confederacy," unpublished manuscript, Oneida Indian Historical Society, Oneida, Wisconsin.

42. Paul Doxtator to President Woodrow Wilson, July 23, 1918, NA, RG 75, Bureau of Indian Affairs, #64300-18-312 (Oneida), CCF 1907–39.

43. Wonderley, *Oneida Iroquois Folklore*, 192–220.

44. Oneida Nation Petition [Jacob Thompson, Ray Elm, Ruth Burr] to President Lyndon B. Johnson, March 26, 1968, Lyndon Johnson Manuscripts, White House Central Files, Box 101, Name Folder "Thompson, Ja," LBJ Presidential Library, Austin, Texas.

45. Jack Campisi and Laurence M. Hauptman, "Talking Back: The Oneida Language and Folklore Project, 1918–1941," *Proceedings of the American Philosophical Society* 125 (December 1981): 441–48; Herbert Lewis, ed., *Oneida Lives* (Lincoln: University of Nebraska Press, 2005).

46. Eric Foner, *Who Owns History? Rethinking the Past in a Changing World* (New York: Hill and Wang, 2002), xv, xvii.

Chapter 4

"Our Future Is Burning Bright"

American Indian Histories as Continuing Stories

Peter Iverson

A century ago most Americans assumed the remaining lands held by American Indians would soon be wrested from indigenous control and that Indian communities would soon be engulfed by non-Indians. Indians would be cast aside, flotsam in the wave of "American progress" washing across the continent. Edward Curtis took a photograph of a group of Navajos on horseback and titled it *The Vanishing Race.* Curtis concluded Indians were entering what he termed the "darkness of an unknown future." Several years later sculptor James Fraser completed *The End of the Trail,* another work not exactly presenting an optimistic view of the Native tomorrow. Given ongoing pressures on Indian lands, it all seemed a matter of time before migrants and immigrants overran these enclaves.[1]

One hundred years later, stereotypes persist; racism remains. But we don't hear a lot about Indians as vanishing peoples. Not only are there more Indians than a century ago, according to the U.S. Census Bureau there are more Navajos today than there were Indians a century ago. And there is greater optimism in many Indian nations about what tomorrow will bring. A recent television public service announcement provided by the Fort McDowell Yavapai Nation noted recent achievements and proclaimed, "Our future is burning bright."[2]

Historians, filmmakers, and other folks you need to watch very carefully shifted from an emphasis on non-Indians as victors, Indians as vanquished, to an emphasis on Indians as victims. In other words, we used to hear bugles and then we began to hear Indian flutes, their echoing lament preparing us for the latest disappointment, the latest disaster. The roles played by Kevin Costner in *Dances With Wolves* to Nicolas Cage in *Windtalkers,* ultimately underlined history being something that happened to Indians rather than being something they made.

Historians should note there is another transition underway in film, with Chris Eyre, Sherman Alexie, and other indigenous writers, directors, and actors combining their talents to create impressive new work. From *Smoke Signals* to *The Fast Runner,* these bold efforts are reaching wider audiences and achieving unparalleled recognition. The success of recently established indigenous film festivals clearly reveals we have entered a new era in this vital medium.[3]

This transformation should encourage historians to reexamine work that we have often included in what we have too casually labeled "Indian history." It has been thirty-five years since Robert F. Berkhofer, Jr., published his call for a new Indian political history. Berkhofer encouraged historians to move toward what he termed an "Indian-centered" history and away from the tired, customary Indian-white relations model. Historians, he observed, still devoted too much attention to non-Indian dreams, expectations, hopes, and priorities. Fred Hoxie's reexamination of *History of Indian-White Relations*, volume 4 of the Smithsonian Institution's *Handbook of North American Indians*, reconfirmed the need to heed Berkhofer's counsel. Published in 1988, it now appears fatally flawed. Hoxie dismisses it as "a Eurocentric artifact."[4]

Some historians have moved away from a preoccupation with federal Indian policy to devote more attention to Indian individuals and communities. These scholars have begun to wade in the murky streams that mark the period from 1900 to 1950. However, much of this solid new work does not proceed past the 1930s and 1940s. Not many historians have been willing to run the rapids of the more recent past. An ongoing fascination with the military campaigns of the nineteenth century should not keep us from perceiving the era, since 1890 contains battlefields of a different sort. Yet we continue to shy away from placing more emphasis on the period since World War II and, with the exception of studies about such topics as Indian gaming and water rights, little investigation has taken place thus far in the 1980s, 1990s, and the first decade of the twenty-first century. If historians are truly going to present the histories of indigenous communities as continuing stories, we are going to have to take our analysis into the here and now.[5]

This same hesitation is reflected in the journals and exhibits sponsored by local and state historical societies. Terms such as discoverer, pioneer, and settler are likely to be restricted to white individuals who lived after Lewis and Clark but before the creation of the Bureau of Reclamation. Pioneers thus can be named Travis but not Todacheene; their last name might be Payne but never Platero. In 1926 the *Chronicles of Oklahoma* published Peter Parnell Duffy's tribute, "The Oklahoma Pioneer." Duffy inflicted one forced rhyme after another on his audience: "he has conquered . . . he has triumphed over all. History will record his great career, and emblazon on the tablets so the future may recall the mighty Oklahoma pioneer." Duffy finished with a flourish: "He has transformed to a paradise each valley, dale, and hill O'er which the noble redman's band once trod. Then teach it to your children of his sacrifice and strife, Burn it in their minds to e'er revere, And on the walls of fame we'll hang a picture of his life, the immortal Oklahoma pioneer."[6]

Western towns established in the latter half of the nineteenth century mirror this preoccupation with the more distant past. City officials in Laramie, Wyoming, for example, seized the opportunity to name the initial streets running from north to south after various U.S. Army generals who had fought against various Indian nations. When I moved to Laramie in 1976, I saw an almost limitless litany of streets honoring Canby and Custer and Gibbon and Harney and Ord and Sheridan and Steele and Sully and Terry and the other usual suspects. I can still hear the voice of a real estate agent, calling me prior to my move to this community, telling me she had found "a cute little house on Custer." I began to have visions of employing a large post office box rather than my home address. "No," I quickly replied. "Absolutely not." I wound up buying a house on Eighth Street.

Given such developments, it is hardly surprising such concepts as dependence or colonialism have been employed to help explain the origins and continuation of poverty, factionalism, and other afflictions. Within the field of American Indian studies, "decolonization" has gained some advocates, especially among individuals who hail from particularly embattled communities. Despite its almost inherent preoccupation with victimization, this kind of analysis can speak to important concerns and can link contemporary perspectives, oral histories, and indigenous languages in significant ways.

Historians have a special opportunity today to tell new stories centered less in loss and more in survival and continuation. The drastic decrease of lands held by various Indian communities during the late nineteenth and early twentieth centuries has been documented in great detail. Without diminishing in any way the difficulties Indians had to confront because of allotment, leasing, sale, and usurpation of their lands, we need to spend more time pondering how Indian communities managed to hold onto as much land as they did. We also should consider more fully indigenous success in places like Arizona, where by executive order many new reservations were established after 1900. This altered emphasis would enable us to move away from the customary dependence on "D" words (such as "death," "decline," "destruction," "deterioration," "division," and "disappearance") to call upon more "R" words: "resilience," "resurgence," "restoration," "renewal," "reappearance," and even "renaissance."[7]

Stories are important in this process. Julie Cruikshank reminds us that stories are more important for what they explain than how many "facts" they bring forth. Stories explain events and reinforce lessons drawn from decisions.

As Keith Basso's work has emphasized, older people will tell stories associated with specific sites in order to encourage proper conduct. AnCita Benally informs us stories help community members remember vital individuals and events from their past. They allow the elders to remind younger people about time-honored values like knowledge, hard work, patience, determination, courage, and achievement.[8]

Indians have demonstrated through time their willingness and ability to create new traditions. Traditions are often marked by symbols that endure, such as the sacred mountains of the Navajos. Speech and silence are symbols, too. How you speak and how comfortable you are with silence will reveal more about you than you initially realize. Indian communities have always placed a value on speaking well.

As the 1960s finally became "the sixties" Indian actions and authorship in the here and now began to push matters forward, ready or not. In 1969 the occupation of Alcatraz by the "Indians of All Tribes" and the publication of Vine Deloria's *Custer Died for Your Sins: An Indian Manifesto* signaled that a new era had begun, one that would have an edge to it, a questioning, searching time period that would shed new light on the past and present. Songwriter Jimmy Curtiss authored lyrics based on Deloria's book, including "Here Come the Anthros," which advised Indians to "hide the past away" because anthropologists were returning "on another holiday." Floyd Westerman soon recorded these songs for an album titled *Custer Died for Your Sins.* On the back of the dust jacket Deloria declared, "With this album the continental divide of oppression is crossed and a new day begins."[9]

That new day expedited the process through which I began to see Indian history more broadly and more completely. I was lucky enough to receive a last-minute invitation to teach at Navajo Community College in that same fateful year of 1969. Living and teaching in the heart of the Navajo Nation, I began to emphasize in my classes the themes of survival, adaptation, and continuity through change. I began to underline how Indian nations had employed a variety of means to transmit values, build communities, foster pride, and nourish families.[10]

The land mattered. The Navajos linked each of their four sacred mountains to a season, a direction, a color, and a valued mineral. Thus Tsoodzil, the mountain non-Indians called Mount Taylor, the Navajos associated with summer, with the south, and with turquoise. Navajo poet Luci Tapahonso later wrote, "Mount Taylor gave us turquoise to honor all men, thus we wear turquoise to honor our brothers, we wear turquoise to honor our sons, we wear turquoise to honor our fathers."[11]

The Navajos believed that the mountains had been placed there for them, that this area constituted the territory in which they were supposed to reside. During treaty negotiations in 1868, federal representative William T. Sherman suggested the Navajos could move to Indian Territory rather than returning to their home country. The head Navajo negotiator, Barboncito, immediately rejected that idea. The Holy People, he replied, did not want the Navajos to live elsewhere, for the Diné had obligations they had to fulfill in that particular place. The treaty of 1868 permitted the Navajos to return to a portion of their homeland. Each year a treaty day holiday is observed. For the Diné, the treaty represented triumph rather than tragedy.[12]

The Navajos have also been noteworthy for their ability to incorporate new traditions into their society. The so-called squash blossom necklace exemplified this capacity. The Navajos noticed the Spaniards and the Mexicans employing silver blossoms for decorative purposes. They created a necklace, combining beads and blossoms. The squash blossoms actually are pomegranate blossoms, and the naja, or "horseshoe," at the base of the necklace is actually a crescent. The necklace became in time quintessentially Navajo, even though its origins could be traced to northern Africa and southern Spain. A comparable story concerns a crescent shaped pastry fashioned initially in southeastern Europe and the Middle East. It became, in time quintessentially French. It is called, of course, a croissant.[13]

Basketball furnishes another example of incorporation. Navajo educator Monty Roessel has determined the five major sports on the Navajo Nation are basketball, basketball, basketball, basketball, and rodeo. You see hoops everywhere. When Tuba City became in 2001 the first high school ever in Arizona to win both the boys' and the girls' championships in consecutive years, probably 99 percent of the community made the trek from the Navajo Nation to the America West Arena in Phoenix.

I learned firsthand about indigenous enthusiasm for the game. I had always been a shooting guard, but new teammates assured me I was a born power forward. In other words, they said, rebound, and pass us the ball. If we could have just played with two or three basketballs simultaneously we might never have lost in tournaments graced with names such as the Sheep Herders Classic.[14]

Even early in the twentieth century one could see Native willingness to review new dimensions and possibilities, to combine, as Tapahonso phrases it, old values and new ideas. In 1922 when the first airplane landed at the recently constructed Flagstaff airport, Navajos showed up in force, carefully checking out this remarkable invention. You can almost hear them in the background asking questions about what they would call in their own language "the car that flies."[15]

Historians can also employ biography to consider continuity and change. "Things have changed and we have changed with them," observed Yavapai physician Carlos Montezuma in the early twentieth century. He resided in Chicago but made the long journey by train to Arizona with increasing frequency during the final years of his life. Local Indian agents perceived him as "an easterner," a term traditionally reserved by westerners for anyone different as well as for anyone residing east of Wahoo, Nebraska. They did not at all applaud the presence of Indians like Montezuma who were better educated, more articulate, and more sophisticated than they were, who gave voice and power to reservation residents. They labeled those Indians who sided with him "the Montezuma crowd," "the Montezuma bunch," "the malcontents," the "long-haired" and "thick-headed Indians," and, my personal favorite, straight out of the second decade of the twentieth century, "the bolsheviki element."[16]

Part of who you are, after all, is who you are not. Rivalries between universities or between one community and another are played out in part on various athletic fields. University of Oklahoma football fans, for example, would say the "N" on the Nebraska football helmets stood for "nowledge," a joke that would be passed along to newcomers and the next generation of Oklahomans. The old rivalries between the Crows and the Lakotas would be carried out in rodeo arenas rather than military battlegrounds.

Throughout the twentieth century, contact and conflict often reinforced one's sense of identity rather than prompting instant assimilation. Tsianina Lomawaima's study of Chilocco Indian School in north-central Oklahoma provides example after example of this generalization. "Indian people at boarding schools," she concludes, "were not passive consumers of an ideology or lifestyle imparted from above by federal administrators . . . an institution founded and controlled by the federal government was inhabited and possessed by those whose identities the institution was committed to erase. Indian people made Chilocco their own. Chilocco was an Indian school."[17]

Again and again we see instances where misguided policies do not result only in disaster. This is not at all to suggest a policy such as termination, which encouraged federal withdrawal from trust responsibilities, constituted a great idea. But it is also to say that threatening times or impending attacks on Indian communities have inspired or pushed various Indian communities to develop their own institutions, including judicial systems whereby members of the nation and, depending on the nature of the case, others could be held accountable for their actions.

Explosive growth in non-Native populations posed problems. Newcomers generally knew little about their new environment and its first occupants. Recent arrivals were also more likely to recreate the environment they left behind. Indigenous peoples understood the scarcity of water in the arid West and the central importance of water in everyday life. That is why, for example, there are so many Navajo communities whose names begin with "To" (the Navajo word for water): Toyei ("scarce water"), Tohatchi ("water is dug out with one's hand"), Toadlena ("water flows up"; a variant spelling), and Tohatin Mesa ("no water mesa"). Can you imagine a developer in Phoenix, Tucson, or Albuquerque employing these phrases for street names? Let's just say it seems rather unlikely. Rather than appreciating a desert environment on its own terms, they saw desert terrain as a lunar landscape waiting for better days, or as that apostle of irrigation William Smythe once put it, "a clean, blank page awaiting the makers of history." Left to their own devices, developers created artificial lakes and other comparable diversions in an effort to make Mesa look more like Minneapolis and Peoria to resemble, well, Peoria. Instead of Tohatin Trail or Toyei Terrace, we confront Key Largo Court and Lobster Trap Lane.[18]

The reservation itself proved to be a key component in Indian survival and continuation. A somewhat curious entity, it embodied Anglo-Americans' desire to achieve assimilation through segregation. Non-Indians sought to convert Indians to Christianity, to teach them the English language, and to own land as individuals. At the same time, they did not want Indians attending their schools or their religious services, and they frowned at the emergence of entrepreneurs like Quanah Parker (Comanche) and Chee Dodge (Navajo).[19]

The attitudes of non-Indians often helped foster results different than had been initially anticipated. In much the same way that prevailing white attitudes ultimately inspired African Americans to establish their own churches and other institutions, American Indians founded comparable entities that yielded avenues for leadership, provided new arenas for achievement, offered outlets for distinctive cultural expressions, goaded individuals to do even better at something than they might have imagined, and reinforced group ties.[20]

It also meant, however, remaining Indian enclaves might have enjoyed rights on paper but not on a prairie; they might have earned water rights through the courts, but, as the attorneys would phrase it, "wet water" remained a distant prospect. Whites still hauled out the same tired argument. They claimed Indians were not taking full advantage of their lands and therefore merited little protection and little support in making their lands more productive. Today we look back and applaud the Supreme Court's decision in *Winters v. U.S.* that created what became known as the Winters' Doctrine; Indians were entitled to access to a water supply sufficient to make possible a more viable reservation economy. However, along the Milk River, the site of this battle over water rights, the Gros Ventres and the Assiniboines who lived on the Fort Belknap Reservation continued to be denied an adequate amount of water.

Indian nations also had their lands reduced in size to create national monuments or had their lands appropriated during wartime for use as gunnery ranges or for the imprisonment of Japanese Americans. During World War II, indigenous people from the Aleutians were transported away from their homes in the rumored wake of Japanese advance; after the war they came back to discover that in their absence American soldiers had stolen their personal property, trashed their homes, and had even ripped off religious icons from their churches.[21]

Shoshone Bannock journalist Mark Trahant recalls his grandfather's allotment being condemned for use during the war and his grandfather being given a check and the assurance that with war's end the land would be returned. But it was not. The army sold the land and adjoining acreage to the city of Pocatello for one dollar, and the site became the Pocatello airport. "The idea that government takes away Indian land is personal in our family," Trahant writes, "not just something that happened in another time to some other people." The transaction could be justified, just as the drowning of lands by new dams in the Dakotas or in upstate New York could be rationalized. The construction of Orme Dam in Arizona would have put most of the land at Fort McDowell under water. A Mesa businessman could not see what all the fuss was about. He dismissed the area as "just a barrio." Fort McDowell at this point in its history was a poor community, but federal, state, and local representatives eventually discovered the Yavapais could not be bought out or shoved out. In southern Idaho, on the other hand, Mark Trahant's grandfather's campaign to regain his land did not succeed. In either instance, as Trahant puts it, "the land has stories to tell."[22]

In the face of indignity and ignorance, Native communities somehow persevered. Older family members somehow believed enough in the future to find ways to keep going in the midst of tremendous adversity. Living in the Navajo Nation I began to learn how Indian nations had employed a

variety of means to transmit values, build or rebuild communities, foster pride, and nourish families. I began to see
Indian histories as continuing stories. As my days in the
Navajo Nation turned into months and the months turned
into years, I gained a more complete understanding of how
determined Indian nations were to pass along key values.
In a time when almost all non-Indians assumed Indian communities would splinter, somehow indigenous individuals
summoned the resolve to invest in that uncertain tomorrow.

One could not learn fully about that resolve exclusively
through archival research. Scholars who wanted to furnish a
more complete picture had to develop new approaches.
Oral histories, traditional teachings, and personal observations had to become part of how historians proceeded. At
the beginning of a new century, however, many students'
indigenous communities remained detached from their sub-
jects, almost as though they concluded by never talking
with Indians and by remaining in distant archives they could
maintain greater objectivity.

Certain centrally important stories might elude them.
Imagine early autumn in Navajo country. The cottonwoods
in Canyon de Chelly have yet to change color, but the
nights are already beginning to turn cold. And that change
of season marked the departure of children for boarding
schools, sometimes hundreds of miles away from home.
Early one morning a Navajo parent wakes up and in a split
second realizes this is the day the bus will come and take
her daughter hundreds of miles away to Intermountain, a
former hospital in northern Utah that had been transformed
into a large boarding school.

She walks deliberately to where her daughter is sleeping and gently awakens her. They gather the daughter's belongings that will accompany her to northern Utah. They leave for the bus stop. Some people are already there. Some parents talk with their children, while others remain silent. Then the bus appears in the distance. Instructions, advice, and reminders are passed along. After her daughter clambers aboard, the bus begins to pull away. The mother watches the bus depart, holds her hands to shade her eyes, and continues to look in that direction even after the bus can no longer be seen.

She then returns home to a too quiet place. The mother realizes again she will not see her daughter for months. She wraps her daughter's voice around her and thinks about the days and months ahead. She becomes all the more determined to work with others to build schools in the Navajo Nation that will keep children from being sent away. "It's time," she says to herself, her voice barely more than a whisper. "It is time for my daughter to come home." In time most Navajo children enrolled in public schools, and today Intermountain is no more.[23]

During the twentieth century historians gave insufficient attention to a variety of occupations and pastimes that reinforced important values in the next generation. Annual tribal fairs and rodeos, for example, grew out of the old agricultural fairs initiated by the federal government early in the twentieth century to show off agricultural achievements of the people and to give the people the chance to hear lectures by professors of agriculture. Although the Bureau of Indian Affairs (BIA) envisioned processions of potatoes and uplifting lectures about lettuce, the Indians appeared generally to be more enthusiastic about horses than horticulture. Jackson Sundown (Nez Perce), Sam Bird-in-Ground (Crow), George Defender (Lakota), and other rodeo stars helped build an audience for rodeo. The Crow Fair soon featured a parade that reflected Crow pride.[24]

At the Eastern Navajo rodeo a few years ago, I noticed the Crownpoint Youth Athletic Association offered fourteen different flavors of snow cones. Immediately impressed by this dazzling array, I wandered over and started copying the list of flavors. A young Navajo woman then walked over and inquired, "Can I help you?" I learned a long while ago in Indian country those four words meant "What in the world are you doing?" I explained I was writing a book on Indian rodeo. She sighed with obvious relief. "Oh, good," she replied. "We thought you might be a food inspector for the Indian Health Service." I wrote that down, too.[25]

The sight of several Navajo Code Talkers at the rodeo prompted me to muse about the extraordinary contribution by Indian nations to the American effort in World War II and to the American military since that era; it is said that 25 percent of all American Indian men are veterans. Twenty-five thousand Native men and women enlisted in the armed forces during World War II, and more than five hundred were killed. An Osage man, Clarence W. Tinker, commanding general of the air forces in Hawaii, lost his life at Midway. The Navajo Code Talkers made a vital difference at Iwo Jima and at other key locations, but recognition for their skills and bravery only came decades after the war ended. And in Hollywood the Code Talkers eventually would be depicted as incapable of proceeding very far without the counsel and intervention of none other than the king of cultural brokers, Nicolas Cage.[26]

At the rodeo I had the opportunity to visit with Bill Kine. He and four other compatriots, each wearing a distinctive, crisp yellow shirt, carried the flags of the Navajo Nation, Arizona, New Mexico, the Eastern Navajo Rodeo Association, and the United States of America into the arena. Members of the Navajo Code Talkers always said they had attempted to defend two nations: the Navajo Nation and the United States. One of the original twenty-nine Code Talkers, artist Carl Gorman, designed a patch for their shirts, which linked the unit with the Hero Twins, who saved the people from monsters.[27]

Conversations with members of Indian nations make evident priorities and concerns. Despite the extraordinary contributions made by Native individuals during World War II, Arizona, New Mexico, and Utah continued to deny Indians who lived on reservations the right to vote. A Navajo soldier in World War II wrote to a BIA official to complain about this denial. Ralph Anderson observed that even with the passage of the Citizenship Act in 1924, Indians still could be blocked at the ballot box. "What kind of citizenship is that?" he asked. Southwestern officials argued since these individuals did not pay property taxes, they should be not allowed to vote. After the war came to an end, many Indian veterans helped push for change. In 1948 Indians finally gained the right to vote in Arizona and New Mexico. In Utah this goal was not achieved until the 1950s.[28]

Such struggles are one component of an ongoing crusade for self-determination. World War II gave many more members of different Indian nations altered perspectives on the utility of education. One compared the lack of an education to a bird attempting to fly without the use of one of its wings. Economic development has also been a crucial concern. Tourism has become very important in the workings of many economies. In the Southwest, for example, the Santa Fe Railway, the Fred Harvey Company, and other interests vigorously promoted travel to the region. In more recent years Indian nations have begun to gain more of a return, as the old-time colonial enterprises have relinquished or been shoved off center stage. From skiing at sunrise on White Mountain Apache to golf at the Mescalero Apaches' Inn of the Mountain Gods to elk hunting at Jicarilla Apache, Indian Country offered attractive destinations long before the advent of casinos. Although the visitors often wore clothing more appropriate for Key West rather than Kayenta and although they sometimes asked the most remarkable questions, they did bring in badly needed dollars and offered inadvertent entertainment. The Navajos watched countless tourists drive miles out of their way in order to reach the Four Corners monument, where the states of Arizona, New Mexico, Utah, and Colorado meet. The Navajos shook their heads slightly as they observed a tourist place his left arm in Utah and his right arm in Colorado, his left leg in Arizona and his right leg in New Mexico. Why did these people do things like this? Why did they ask the person being photographed to say "cheese"?[29]

Those Indian nations enjoying economic revitalization have generally not forgotten time-honored values like generosity. The Fort McDowell Yavapai Nation, for example, has contributed generously to Arizona's universities for programs supporting Indian students. Peterson Zah, a former president of the Navajo Nation, has served for many years as a special advisor to the Arizona State University president and has worked tirelessly to increase Navajo and Indian enrollment, retention, and graduation. He feels strongly about this matter, in part because of his own life experience. In the 1950s, as he neared graduation from the Phoenix Indian School, Zah expressed an interest in going on to college. Teachers and counselors at Phoenix Indian School tried to discourage him, telling him he did not need to go to college because he had been trained as a carpenter. Zah wound up getting a partial athletic scholarship to play basketball at Phoenix College and then transferred to Arizona State and graduated with a degree in education. As commencement neared he sent invitations to attend the ceremony to all the folks at Phoenix Indian School who had advised him not to go on to college. "You know," he says, his face producing simultaneously a grin and a grimace, "no one came."[30]

Today more than seven hundred Navajo students and seven hundred additional Indian students attend Arizona State University. At the end of each semester graduating students are honored through a special ceremony in Gammage Auditorium. It is a wonderful occasion. Elders, parents, younger siblings, and babies are all there to honor the graduates, who often are the first person in their family to complete this complicated journey. Peterson Zah never misses that gathering.[31]

Countless Indian women and men have found ways to believe in, invest in, and build for the future. As Vine Deloria, Jr., has observed, it is time for American historians to pay attention to that struggle. "The ignorance of historians" of the twentieth century, he grumbled, "has to be a studied ignorance, a teeth-gnashing determination to concentrate on familiar topics to the exclusion of reality, if necessary." Too many students of the American past, he groaned, "can tell us precisely what Lewis and Clark had for breakfast on the Bitterroot in 1804 but are unable to even guess what happened to Indians following the Indian Citizenship Act of 1924, or to name the current chairman of the tribe they profess immense expertise and knowledge about."[32]

The past and present of Indian peoples remind us that American Indian history is centrally important but it is not always linear. There can be circles, too. During the mid-nineteenth century, the Pimas and the Maricopas who lived near the Gila River enjoyed stability and prosperity because of their success as farmers. They graciously and generously fed outsiders who came through the area en route to the gold fields of California. A generation later, white newcomers began their own farms. Their dams and ditches upstream eventually dried up most of the Indians' water resources. Gila River persisted with farming operations, starting Gila River Farms in 1968. Today Gila River Farms devotes roughly sixteen thousand acres to cotton, alfalfa, wheat, and citrus, but the Arizona Water Settlement Act of 2005 will allow the Pima-Maricopas to expand and revitalize their operations.[33]

Many Indian nations are attempting to build from the foundation of the casinos to encourage people to come to stay for a longer time or to attract the same visitors more frequently. Gila River, for example, now claims three casinos: Wild Horse Pass, Vee Quiva, and Lone Butte. It offers the Sheraton Wild Horse Pass Resort and Spa, the Koli Equestrain Center, the Whirlwind Golf Club, the Wild Horse

Pass Business Park, and the Huhugam Heritage Center. The Heritage Center is in its early stages of development, but it is an impressive structure. And in a pleasingly ironic development Gila River is now the new home for Rawhide, an Old West theme park that got squeezed out of Scottsdale. As the inexorable wave of red tile roofs came closer and closer, the owners of Rawhide opted for relocation.[34]

There are other circles, too. In the rural counties of the Dakotas, eastern Montana, Nebraska, and Kansas, census data records that many young non-Indians are leaving the area. Their departure has been fueled by a changing farming and ranching economy, boredom, and a perception that life in the city will offer more dollars and more diversions. In the county in eastern Kansas that my mother's family migrated to in the 1860s and 1870s, the population in 1900 reached twenty-five thousand. Today it is about eight thousand. In addition, today members of long-time ranching and farming families are being lambasted by urban-based environmentalists who say that such families are not using the land properly or productively. As many leave, Indians often are coming home to a place where many have never lived or lived only briefly.

Through work that combines archival research, oral histories, traditional teachings, and personal observation, historians can make vital contributions to a truly new American Indian history. We must, as Vine Deloria, Jr., wrote, "bring historical consciousness of the whole Indian story to full light in order to regain the values which we cherish and admire from the heroic past. We can do no less for this generation and for the generations coming after us than to give them a sense of reality which can only come to people with a history."[35]

There are many important questions confronting American Indian nations today. Diabetes is taking a terrible toll. In many communities the percentage of Native language speakers continues to decline. Given all the terrible things Native persons and nations have had to confront and endure for hundreds of years, the notion of a new day is greeted with considerable, understandable, and appropriate caution. Times may be better now in many Indian nations, but there is also a common understanding that the future is always fragile. Prosperity is not a given; tomorrow will arrive without guarantees. But there is little talk today about vanishing. Throughout Indian country there is talk instead about new horizons to explore.[36] There is consistent affirmation of Acoma poet Simon Ortiz's belief that "the People shall continue." In one indigenous community after another there is a future "burning bright."[37]

Notes

This essay is dedicated to the memory of D'Arcy McNickle and Bob Thomas. McNickle served as director of the Newberry Library's Center for American Indian History during its first years (1973–77). As a member of the center's advisory board, Thomas offered counsel to graduate and postgraduate students who had gained Indian history fellowships at the Newberry in the 1970s. I held a doctoral fellowship at the center and eventually served on the advisory board for a decade. As always, I thank my many indigenous teachers through the years for all they have taught me.

    1. Brian Dippie, *The Vanishing American: White Attitudes and U.S. Indian Policy* (Middletown, Conn.: Wesleyan University Press, 1982), 209.

2. The Fort McDowell Yavapai Nation exemplifies the greatly improved economic picture in some Indian communities. For a concise study of Fort McDowell's evolution, see Jeffrey Sparks, "The Fort McDowell Yavapai Nation in the 20th Century" (master's thesis, Arizona State University, Tempe, 2006).

3. For an engaging overview of recent developments in American Indian film, see Adam Bayes, "The American Indian Film Festival and the Indigenous Film and Arts Festival: Vehicles for Expression in the Changing World of Native Cinema" (master's thesis, Arizona State University, Tempe, 2006).

4. Robert F. Berkhofer, Jr., "The Political Context of a New Indian History," *Pacific Historical Review* 40 (August 1971): 357–82. Hoxie's conclusions are brought forth in an essay, "Missing the Point: Academic Experts and American Indian Politics," included in a volume on Indian politics and activism since 1900 edited by Daniel M. Cobb and Loretta Fowler, forthcoming from the University of Nebraska Press.

5. For portraits of Philip Martin, Wilma Mankiller, and other indigenous leaders of the twentieth century, see R. David Edmunds, ed., *The New Warriors: Native American Leaders Since 1900* (Lincoln: University of Nebraska Press, 2001).

6. Peter Parnell Duffy, "The Oklahoma Pioneer," *The Chronicles of Oklahoma* 4, no. 2 (June 1926): 201.

7. Ak-Chin, Camp Verde, Cocopah, Fort McDowell, Pascua Yaqui, Payson, Prescott, and Tohono O'odham were all established after 1900. About 28 percent of the land in Arizona is officially Indian land.

8. Julie Cruikshank, *The Social Life of Stories: Narrative and Knowledge in the Yukon Territory* (Lincoln: University of Nebraska Press, 1998); Keith Basso, *Wisdom Sits in Places: Language and Landscape among the Western Apache* (Albuquerque: University of New Mexico Press, 1996); AnCita Benally, "Hane Bee'ehaniih: With Stories It Is Remembered" (master's thesis, Arizona State University, Tempe, 1993).

9. Vine Deloria, Jr., *Custer Died for Your Sins: An Indian Manifesto* (New York: Macmillan, 1969); Floyd Westerman, album, *Custer Died for Your Sins,* 1969.

10. See Peter Iverson, "I May Connect Time," in *The American Indian and the Problem of History,* ed. Calvin Martin (New York: Oxford University Press, 1987), 136–43.

11. Luci Tapahonso, "This Is How They Were Placed for Us," in *Blue Horses Rushed In: Stories and Poems* (Tucson: University of Arizona Press, 1997), 39–42.

12. See Peter Iverson, *Diné: A History of the Navajos* (Albuquerque: University of New Mexico Press, 2002), 63–65.

13. Ibid., 32.

14. Iverson, "I May Connect Time."

15. A photograph of this encounter may be found in the William H. Switzer Collection, Cline Library, Northern Arizona University, Flagstaff. This image is included in Peter Iverson, ed., *"For Our Navajo People": Diné Letters, Speeches, and Petitions, 1900–1960* (Norman: University of Oklahoma Press, 2002), 260.

16. Peter Iverson, *Carlos Montezuma and the Changing World of American Indians* (Albuquerque: University of New Mexico Press, 2001), 130–35.

17. Tsianina Lomawaima, *They Called It Prairie Light: The Story of Chilocco Indian School* (Lincoln: University of Nebraska Press, 1994), 167.

18. The Navajo place names are from Laurence D. Linford, *Navajo Places: History, Legends, Landscape* (Salt Lake City: University of Utah Press, 2000).

19. The life and times of Quanah Parker have gained the attention of biographers. See, e.g., William T. Hagan, *Quanah Parker, Comanche Chief* (Norman: University of Oklahoma Press, 1992), and Bill Neeley,

The Last Comanche Chief: The Life and Times of Quanah Parker (New York: John Wiley and Sons, 1995).

20. Peter Iverson, *"We Are Still Here": American Indians in the Twentieth Century* (Wheeling, Ill.: Harlan Davidson, 1998): 105–13; author's personal observation.

21. See, e.g., Dean Kohlhoff, *When the Wind Was a River: Aleut Evacuation in World War II* (Seattle: University of Washington Press, 1995).

22. Mark Trahant, "Creating Sacred Places," *National Museum of the American Indian* (Spring 2005): 32–34.

23. Iverson, *Diné*, 232–33.

24. For a discussion of the Crow Nation in the early twentieth century, see Frederick Hoxie, *Parading through History: The Crow Nation in America, 1805–1935* (Cambridge: Cambridge University Press, 1995).

25. Peter Iverson and Linda MacCannell, *Riders of the West: Portraits from Indian Rodeo* (Seattle: University of Washington Press, 1999), 48.

26. See (or rather, don't see) the film *Windtalkers*, dir. John Woo, Lion Rock Productions, 2002.

27. Iverson, *Riders of the West*, 48–49.

28. Peter Iverson, ed., *"For Our Navajo People": Diné Letters, Speeches, and Petitions, 1900–1960* (Albuquerque: University of New Mexico Press, 2002), 144–45.

29. Iverson, *Diné*, 223–25; Iverson, "For Our Navajo People," 95; Myla Vicenti Carpio and Peter Iverson, "'The Inalienable Right to Govern Ourselves': Wendell Chino and the Struggle for Indian Self-Determination in New Mexico," in *New Mexican Lives: Profiles and Historical Studies,* ed. Richard W. Etulain (Albuquerque: University of New Mexico Press, 2002), 265–84.

30. Peterson Zah, presentation to graduate seminar in American Indian history, Arizona State University, Tempe, 2001.

31. Peterson Zah received an honorary degree from Arizona State University in 2005.

32. Vine Deloria, Jr., "The Twentieth Century," in *Red Men and Hat Wearers: Viewpoints in Indian History,* ed. Daniel Tyler (Boulder, Colo.: Pruett, 1977). See also Robert White, *Tribal Assets: The Rebirth of Indian America* (New York: Henry Holt, 1990), and Edmunds, *New Warriors.*

33. Judy Nichols, "Water Deal Allows Gila Tribe to Renew Tradition of Farming," *Arizona Republic,* January 19, 2005: A1.

34. Author's personal observation; "Gila River Indian Community Profile," *Native Peoples: Art and Lifeways* (March–April 2005): 33–48; Betty Beard, "Flavor of Life on Reservation: Resort's Concierge Paints Picture of Gila River Culture," *Arizona Republic,* February 23, 2005.

35. Deloria, "Twentieth Century."

36. Iverson, *"We Are Still Here,"* 208–209.

37. Simon Ortiz, *Continuance,* tour booklet for the Pueblo Cultural Center in Albuquerque, New Mexico.

Chapter 5

Wilma's Jingle Dress

Ojibwe Women and Healing in the
Early Twentieth Century

Brenda J. Child

I was fortunate to meet Wilma Mankiller a number of years ago when I was an assistant professor of history and she was a guest speaker on the college campus where I taught. Over dinner that evening, she told me about an interesting visit she paid to my community, the Red Lake Reservation in northern Minnesota. Red Lake has an unusual history among tribes in the United States, unique even from other Ojibwe bands, because our people managed to stay on our ancestral lands throughout the tumult of the nineteenth century, and the reservation was never allotted. To this day, Red Lake remains communally owned Indian Country, and our hereditary chiefs work as partners in tribal affairs alongside elected officials. Wilma came to northern Minnesota at the invitation of Roger Jourdain, Red Lake's legendary tribal chairman first elected in 1959, still in office when Wilma became principal chief in the 1980s. Wilma came in January, not a time of year when we usually have many visitors from Oklahoma. Chairman Jourdain must have been impressed, because Wilma mentioned that he presented her with gifts that included a jingle dress. The chairman's gesture was perfect, because the jingle dress is a strong cultural reference to the power of women.

The jingle dress is an Ojibwe tradition that began in the early twentieth century, but one with enduring significance. Ojibwe people associate the jingle dress with therapeutic rituals that support physical and spiritual healing. In every part of community and economic life related to the well-being of families and health, Ojibwe women were especially active, and the jingle dress and rituals associated with it are part of their legacy. Women demonstrated an extraordinary commitment to good life and health, even during the post-allotment turmoil, through continued dedication to ceremonial life, indigenous forms of healing, and perhaps most dynamically as laborers in the traditional economy.

Ojibwe women engaged their changing world straight on. They adapted gender roles and expectations and adjusted labor practices to the new circumstances of the reservation. Women worked as healers within their communities and practiced what today we call holistic medicine. Their vocation allowed the most proficient individuals to identify and gather plants for everyday and occasional use for a range of conditions. Women continued to harvest food, just as they had in the pre-reservation era. Wild rice and maple syrup are examples of the bounty of women's labor. Women worked as the principal harvesters of wild rice in their communities, bringing good health and stability to Ojibwe life in years otherwise notable for land loss, deprivation, and crisis.

The Jingle Dress Dance flourished under harsh conditions in the Great Lakes area. Ojibwe women applied the ceremony like a salve to fresh wounds. They designed jingle dresses, organized sodalities, and danced at tribal gatherings, large and intimate, spreading a new tradition while participating in innovative rituals of healing. Women nurtured the body and spirit with food, medicines, and dance. In the midst of turmoil during the post-allotment era, as people looked for ways to reorder their chaotic worlds, the Jingle Dress Dance was dream-given to the Ojibwe people.

The Jingle Dress Dance first appeared around World War I. Special healing songs are associated with the jingle dress, and both songs and dresses possess a strong therapeutic value. Women who participate in the Jingle Dress Dance and wear these special dresses do so to ensure the health and well-being of an individual, family, or even the broader tribal community. The jingle dress is a frequent theme in contemporary storytelling among Ojibwes, and one narrative in particular addresses its origin. The setting for the story is sometimes in the Mille Lacs Ojibwe community in north-central Minnesota, in others at White Fish Bay, Ontario. Both communities express a great devotion to traditional Ojibwe song and dance.

The following story is the one I learned at Red Lake about the origin of the Jingle Dress Dance: In the era of World War I, perhaps a result of the widespread epidemic of Spanish influenza, an Ojibwe girl became very sick. Her father, fearing the worst, sought a vision to save her life, and this was how he learned of a unique dress and dance. The father made this dress for his daughter and asked her to dance a few springlike steps, in which one foot was never to leave the ground. Before long, she felt stronger and continued the dance. After her recovery, she continued to dance in the special dress, and eventually formed the first Jingle Dress Dance Society.[1]

Ojibwe narratives recount that a man conceived the Jingle Dress Dance after receiving a vision, though women were responsible for its proliferation. Traditionally, a man who experienced a particularly strong vision often shared it with other people, and sometimes with the community at large. In Ojibwe culture, women typically did not seek visions because spiritual power came to them at menarche. Men and women both had dreams that assisted them in healing. Stories suggest that the first jingle dress dancer was a young girl, yet females of all ages, from youths to elders, historically embraced the tradition.

The jingle dress tradition coincided with a new round of suppression of Indian religion in the United States, as the Dance Order from Washington arrived in 1921.[2] There is little doubt that Ojibwe women disregarded the new ruling because historic photographs show them in jingle dresses from around 1920 and every decade thereafter, first on reservations and even later in the cities. When the jingle dress was introduced it was an innovation but one consistent with Ojibwe spiritual practices and traditions of song and dance. The Jingle Dress Dance movement was in effect anticolonial because the new social practice organized and flourished under the Indian Office ban on ritualistic dance.[3]

Jingle dress dancing holds a spiritual power for Ojibwe people because of its association with healing. Since World War I, the tradition spread throughout Ojibwe Country and soon after reached our Dakota neighbors. Dakota women added their own artistic flourishes and social processes. Dakota communities such as Fort Totten in North Dakota, who maintain enduring ties of friendship and culture to the Ojibwes at Red Lake, have taken great pride in their Jingle Dress Dance tradition. Dakota women have worn jingle dresses at the Red Lake powwow every summer for several generations.

In the world of the Ojibwes, spiritual power moves through air. Sounds hold significance.[4] The jingle dress is special because of the rows of metal cones, *ziibaaska'iganan* in the Ojibwe language, that dangle from the garment's fabric to produce a pleasantly dissonant rattle as they bounce against one another. The effect is greater when many women dance together. When jingle dresses first appeared, they resembled women's ceremonial dresses of the era, but the rows of jingles were new. Innovation is always a part of powwow and dance regalia, and the jingle dress is no exception, but dresses through the decades share many common features.

The Minnesota Historical Society has a dress from the early twentieth century in their collection. Designed by Mary Bigwind of the White Earth Reservation, the jingle dress belonged to her granddaughter Madeline when she was a teenager. It is a sleeveless, black velvet dress with an empire waist. A single line of jingles is in a neat row at the bodice, hip, knee, and hemline. The jingles are fashioned from round snuff can lids pressed into the distinctive shape of cones. Dancers often completed their ensemble with a belt. My grandmother and older women at Red Lake wore rather simple jingle dresses at powwows some fifty years after its introduction, well before the great jingle dress revival that began in the 1980s, when interest in the dress grew along with the contest powwow and expansion of the northern and southern circuits. The jingle dress evolved into a stylish, elaborate pan-Indian phenomenon, but for Ojibwe people it persists as a ceremonial dress with specific cultural associations.[5]

Anthropologists Patricia Albers and Beatrice Medicine witnessed the "sudden explosion and spread of jingle dresses and dancing" that took place on the powwow circuit in the 1980s. In fact, they cited the jingle dress trend as one reason it is challenging for scholars to write about the powwow, which is an "ever-changing and expanding world" with both "enormous changes" as well as "persisting traditions."[6] Tara Browner, an ethnomusicologist of Choctaw ancestry, writes about her own experience of being a jingle dress dancer on the powwow circuit for seven years in her study *Heartbeat of the People: Music and Dance of the Northern Pow-wow.* Browner writes about the reverence she has for the "ever-unfolding" Jingle Dress Dance tradition:

> The very act of dancing in this dress constitutes a prayer for healing, and often spectators, musicians, and other dancers will make gifts of tobacco to a dancer and request that she pray for an ill family member while she dances. An example of hidden spirituality and ritual within a public forum, the ever-unfolding story of the Jingle Dress Dance is unique in Indian Country. There is little fanfare and no

public announcement when the Jingle Dance is performed as a healing prayer, only a quiet circulation of family members from dancer to dancer, a whispered request, and a quick nod of thanks by both parties.[7]

Today scholars also view the Jingle Dress Dance tradition as an ever-unfolding movement in the ever-changing way American Indians create and adapt the powwow to new circumstances. As Albers and Medicine have explained, "songs, styles of singing and dancing, and regalia designs unique to particular tribes and regions are now crossing cultural boundaries more and more often."[8] Many American Indian people appreciate the Jingle Dress Dance tradition as a prayer of healing, and its widespread adoption by other tribal women, especially since the 1980s, suggests that people from all over Native North America find power and meaning in its ceremonial performance.[9]

The introduction of the jingle dress rallied a communal spirit among Ojibwe people, a spirit that sustains Indian people of diverse tribal backgrounds today. The Jingle Dress Dance began as a creative approach to adversity, illness, and poor health, with a foundation solidly rooted in traditional Ojibwe song and dance. The Spanish influenza pandemic was a deadly peril when the tradition was new, sickening Indians on reservations and children in government boarding schools. By the time of the 1918 outbreak, tuberculosis had replaced smallpox as the largest health threat to Indians and the number of TB patients on reservations, in boarding schools, and in sanatoriums multiplied. Trachoma was also pervasive. The highly contagious eye disease was not deadly, but it caused misery and suffering for otherwise healthy children and families. It first appeared in government boarding schools before afflicting the general Indian population in disproportionate numbers.[10] Ojibwe women, perhaps more than ever, found their special knowledge of healing in demand.

Government physicians trivialized the medical expertise of Ojibwe women, though women persisted in their work. Doctors, confounded by the dismal state of health in Indian communities, blamed Indian families for creating unsanitary living conditions and contributing to high rates of tuberculosis and other diseases, while they asserted their own ideas and approaches to the body, health, and disease. The Ojibwe method of health and wellness, which linked the physical body to spiritual and emotional health, came under attack in the reservation period, as critics charged that these beliefs held Indians back from assimilation and racial advance.

Dr. Thomas Rodwell traveled to the rather remote Red Lake Reservation in northern Minnesota in the early twentieth century. As the agency's physician, he shared the outlook of his contemporaries in government service, most of whom had little appreciation for the skill of Native healers. Rodwell made no mention of their work when he addressed the problem of tuberculosis and smallpox in the Red Lake community in a narrative to Washington in 1906. Red Lake's physician, living closer to the agency seventy-five miles away, made only sporadic visits to the Indian community. Rodwell's reports to Washington reflected shortcomings characteristic of the profession of agency doctor, chief among them a limited experience with and disdain for the medicinal and spiritual practices in the Indian communities where they worked. Rodwell was pleased to discover that most members of the Red Lake community did not resist Western medical interventions and were amenable to his services.[11]

Red Lake people, relentlessly pragmatic, accepted Western medicine, adding it to their long-standing repertoire of indigenous healing. Rodwell misinterpreted the willingness of Red Lake people to visit the doctor as a sign of cultural submission. In a triumphant communication to his supervisors, he proclaimed a moral victory over traditional spiritual practices at Red Lake. Rodwell wrote to Washington, "The Indians under my professional charge have now almost entirely given up their grand medicine ideas and are availing themselves of the professional services and remedies of the Agency physician."[12]

Rodwell never imagined Ojibwe women who worked with plants and medicines beyond his gaze as fellow medical practitioners, though he could see the utility of Euroamerican field matrons. He requested that Washington assign recruits to northern Minnesota, confident that field matrons might be "of very great comfort and welfare of the women and children and the sick."[13] Five years later, a staff of field matrons worked among the Ojibwes in Minnesota. One person hired was Josephine Bonga, an Ojibwe woman of mixed ancestry. Field matrons assigned to the Great Lakes had direct contact with the community, more so than the agency physicians, and Bonga and her colleagues held complex and nuanced opinions of Ojibwe families. Day-to-day experiences within Ojibwe homes taught them to appreciate the valuable contributions women made to community health.

As other scholars have noted, field matrons also documented the social life of Indian communities in the early twentieth century.[14] Bonga provided rich details in her written surveys about tribal economies, household conditions, family life, and health. She witnessed Ojibwe survival through years of intense hardship. Bonga and other field matrons came face to face with sickness, disability, and poverty, but they also noted the considerable efforts of Ojibwe labor. In particularly vivid detail, they described women's work at fishing, blueberry and cranberry picking, gardening, making maple sugar, and wild rice gathering. Field matrons were among the first health care workers to warn of the threat posed by returned boarding school students, who appeared to be the main carriers of tuberculosis and trachoma within Ojibwe communities. Bonga and her colleagues would have been aware of the persistence of tribal spiritual traditions—that Ojibwe people had not given up their grand medicine ideas.

There were other intelligent observers of Ojibwe life in the early reservation era. Frances Densmore carried out fieldwork among my people in the early twentieth century. A brilliant ethnomusicologist, Densmore began researching Ojibwe music in 1905, when she made her first trip to the Grand Portage Reservation on Lake Superior in northern Minnesota. She worked with Ojibwe people and studied them throughout her long life until her death in 1957 at the age of ninety. As a young woman, Densmore attended Oberlin Conservatory of Music, was deeply impressed with pioneer ethnographer Alice Fletcher's work on Omaha music, and knew something about Dakota culture from her years growing up in Red Wing, Minnesota.[15] Her collaborations in the field with Ojibwe people at Leech Lake, Red Lake, and White Earth in 1906–1909 allowed Densmore to transcend her limited education, mature as a scholar, and carve out a place for herself within the new discipline of anthropology. By the time she published her first major study, *Chippewa Music,* in 1910, Densmore was already a professional collaborator with the Bureau of American Ethnology, a position she held until 1957.[16]

Early on, Densmore appreciated that Ojibwe people organize their world with plants and music coexisting in symbiotic partnership. Already a passionate student of Indian music, Densmore found that her fieldwork made her increasingly attentive to Ojibwe plant knowledge. Densmore eventually made trips to most of Minnesota's Ojibwe reservations, as well as to Lac Court Oreilles in Wisconsin and to Manitou Rapids in Ontario. Her fieldwork resulted in a breakthrough discussion of American Indian ethnobotany that she titled "Uses of Plants by the Chippewa Indians." Exposure to the Ojibwe worldview taught Densmore to appreciate the relationship between Ojibwe use of plants in their natural environment and the Ojibwe people's musical tradition. True to her education in Ojibwe Country, Densmore explained to her colleagues, "Herbs were used in the treatment of the sick and in the working of charms, and songs were sung to make the treatment and the charms effective," referring colleagues to her earlier music articles on music published in the reports.[17]

After her landmark trip in 1905, Densmore engaged in two astonishingly productive decades of fieldwork, when she interacted with women in particular. Essential to interpreting her field experiences, published work, and scholarly legacy today is the recognition that more than half of the sixty-three people she named as informants for her articles about Ojibwe plant knowledge were women. In "Uses of

Plants" Densmore wrote, "A majority of the informants on this subject were women," acknowledging that "both men and women related the uses of plants in medicine, economic life, and the useful and decorative arts."[18]

As informants, interpreters, and friends, Ojibwe women contributed significantly to Densmore's successful career. Mary Warren English, who lived on the White Earth Reservation, played a critical role in a decade and a half of Densmore's fieldwork. English served as Densmore's principal interpreter beginning in 1907 and facilitated Densmore's fieldwork for the next fifteen years. While working as an interpreter, she introduced Densmore to many of the remarkable practitioners of holistic medicine in Ojibwe communities. English had many contacts at Red Lake, where she taught school for fifteen years and married her husband, John. Her home, White Earth, was rich in medicinal herbs, making it an ideal location for Densmore to acquire plant specimens.

Densmore was fortunate to gain the friendship of Mary Warren English—and that of her remarkable family. The Warrens of White Earth were a family of French, English, and Ojibwe ancestry with a long history at Madeline Island, named for their grandmother.[19] Descendants of White Crane, the hereditary chief at LaPointe, they had arrived at White Earth during the removals of 1868–70. Mary Warren English was one of six children; her brother was the extraordinary nineteenth-century historian William W. Warren, author of *History of the Ojibway People*.[20]

Densmore acknowledged the influence of the extended Warren family in her published works. Densmore recalled first

meeting Julia Spears Warren after returning to White Earth
for their annual tribal celebration held on June 14, 1907:

> After a few days at the rectory we were invited to the home
> of Mrs. Charles W. Mee, a niece of William W. Warren, the
> historian of the tribe. There we remained more than two
> weeks while I wrote down Chippewa stories and became
> acquainted with the Indians. Too much appreciation can
> not be expressed for the aid and encouragement given by
> Mrs. Mee and her mother, Mrs. Julia Warren Spears, at
> that time and throughout my work. Mrs. Mee helped me
> contact the Indians, often acting as interpreter, her mother
> related many incidents of historic interest, and her aunt,
> Mrs. Mary Warren English, was my principal interpreter
> for more than ten years in my work for the Bureau of
> American Ethnology.[21]

In Ojibwe Country, Densmore encountered a dynamic net-
work of women who specialized in plants and their healing
properties. At White Earth, Red Lake, and elsewhere in
northern Minnesota she grew to appreciate the particular
knowledge of women while she organized and classified the
dozens of plants and herbs they gathered. It makes sense
that many of the plants Ojibwe women gathered were exclusive to female health issues and wellness. In fact, seventeen
of the nearly two hundred plants Densmore identified by
their botanical and Ojibwe names were described as medicines for "female diseases," according to her informants. A
number of other plants treated menstrual discomforts. One,
black cohosh, is prescribed by physicians today and widely

used by women in North America and Europe for relief of menopause complaints. Densmore found that Ojibwe women used this same plant for female health.[22]

Medicine people harvested many plants in August, *manoo-minikie giizis,* the ricing month in the northern Great Lakes. A plant was picked for its roots, stems, or leaves to make *mashki akeeng,* or medicine. The Ojibwe approach to wellness linked the body to spiritual and emotional health, a worldview appreciated by very few westerners who encountered American Indians living on reservations in the early twentieth century.

Ojibwe people regard plants as sacred because of their ability to nourish and heal the body. In Ojibwemowin, our language, the term for medicine is strength of the earth, or *mashkiki.* Medicine people approached plant and medicinal knowledge in a meticulously systematic way, always emphasizing, as Densmore put it, "experiment and study." Like artists in their work, they were masterful observers of the natural world. They knew the exact time to harvest a multiplicity of plants, a quantity of which had the most ephemeral season. They understood the correct part of the plant to use, even recognizing the importance of compounding plants for medicines in some cases.

Densmore learned that Ojibwe people liked to augment their diets with a variety of wild plants, many of which were vitamin rich and consumed as teas. Ojibwe people especially liked teas made from the twigs of wild cherry, chokecherry, and red raspberry, or the leaves of wintergreen spruce or snowberry, which they sweetened with maple sugar. Densmore was served a simple Ojibwe beverage of maple sugar dissolved in cold water, which she found "pleasantly refreshing" during a warm summer day in the field. She found that Ojibwe people were also very fond of "swamp tea," which is appreciated for calming stomach ailments, preferring it still to many of the perhaps more convenient remedies found in drugstores or Indian health clinics. Swamp tea, which Ojibwe people also refer to as *muckigobug,* commonly called Labrador tea, has the added benefit of vitamin C.[23]

After Densmore met the healer Nawajibigokwe, she commented, "Few persons on the White Earth Reservation are more skilled than she in the lore of native medicines." Indeed, Nawajibigokwe was highly regarded in her community for gathering minisinowuck, or island herb medicine, traditionally given to departing warriors. Nawajibigokwe, whose name Densmore translated as "Woman Dwelling in the Midst of the Rocks," composed songs related to this herb. Densmore noted that while Ojibwe people had a number of commonly accepted designations for plants and trees in their environment, "individuals often had their own names for the plants which they used as remedies." Healers sometimes did not reveal a particular plant's name to Densmore.[24]

Densmore visited the most remote of all the Minnesota Indian communities in 1918. Ponemah rises from the water at the point where the upper and lower portions of Red Lake join, forming a vast freshwater lake in northern Minnesota. In Ponemah Densmore witnessed firsthand the Ojibwe way of life, and her ability to appreciate the rich existence she discovered there outpaced the intransigence of her contemporaries who also worked with Ojibwe people. An Indian agent assigned to Red Lake in the early twentieth century had little regard for the "ugly lot" of pagans at Ponemah but still managed to admire "the remarkable resources of their country."[25] He visited Red Lake in the middle of the summer and observed the abundance of the Ojibwe seasonal economy at the turn of the century:

> Even at this season they have unlimited supplies of rasp-
> berries, blueberries, and gooseberries, nearly all of them
> have gardens and have raised more vegetables than they
> can possibly use, which they have no means of disposing
> of. There is an immense growth of timber which is useful
> for poles, posts, and cord wood and would be readily
> saleable if they had some means of getting it to market.
> The supply of fish and game is practically unlimited, the
> whole peninsula being a famous hunting ground for
> moose and deer. They also get many furs and have a few
> good hay meadows. These resources they keep to them-
> selves and will not permit any white men or any other
> Indians to participate in them, but for lack of market they
> of course utilize a very small fraction of it.[26]

In 1918 Ponemah was only accessible by water or by crossing over the frozen ice in winter. Densmore, inspired by the dynamic traditions of Ojibwe music she discovered there, recorded many songs that deeply influenced her ideas about American Indian music and its relationship to healing and medicine. She later wrote about the isolated community, "Most of the Indians are members of the Midewiwin and its rites are closely observed." After Ponemah, Densmore con-sistently underscored in her writings and lectures that Ojibwe people believe in "the healing power of music." Densmore came to regard her Ojibwe informants, in her words, as "primitive psychologists," because of their ability to harness the spiritual energy of song for emotional health.[27]

As an ethnographer, Densmore learned to appreciate Ojibwe culture and values through careful study of their plants, medicine, and music. She understood that "health and long life represented the highest good to the mind of the Chippewa, and he who had knowledge conducive to that end was the most highly esteemed among them."[28] In the Great Lakes, *manoomin,* or wild rice, is the supreme plant, respected in ceremony and daily life. Densmore's "Uses of Plants" presented an unusually rich ethnography of the traditional wild rice harvest in the Great Lakes, which she explored in other publications, including *Chippewa Customs* (1929).

When Densmore visited Ojibwe Country, the traditional wild rice harvest was primarily the domain of women; not until a few decades later did men take over primary responsibility for ricing. Her study thus captures a profoundly different historic era in Ojibwe history when women still controlled the traditional harvest. As well Densmore attentively described the details of harvesting, from preharvest binding of the stalks together to the multiple steps of postharvest processing. Densmore concluded simply, "The rice was harvested by the women," and her valuable photographs capture Ojibwe women at every stage of production.[29]

Densmore observed a similarly important role for Ojibwe women in maple syrup cultivation. Women set up seasonal camps, where they put in as many as twelve hundred to two thousand taps in large stands of maple trees, to render great quantities of watery sap to its amber liquid form every spring. Densmore, fascinated by this annual event, described the Ojibwe sugar bush in vivid ethnographic detail. Even before other family members came to the sugar bush, the women had carefully prepared for the cheerful labor of making maple syrup. Densmore wrote:

> Arriving at the camp, the women shoveled the snow away from the sugar lodge and soon made themselves comfortable. A ladder of tree branches was among the articles stored during the winter, and placing this against the framework of the lodge they ascended and spread their rolls of birch bark on the roof. On the platforms in the interior of the lodge they spread cedar boughs, if such were available, and on these were laid rush mats, over which were spread blankets and warm furs. The storehouse was opened, the great rolls of birch bark being turned back, one at a time, until beneath the weather-worn coverings were seen the heaps of bark dishes, makuks, and buckets, white outside and warm yellow within, others a soft gray or dulled by age to a rich mahogany color. The odor of balsam and dry sweet birch bark came from the lodge. There was also a supply of birch bark for making new utensils, if such were necessary. The material which the women brought with them from the winter camps depended, of course, on their knowledge of what had been left in the storing lodge the previous season.[30]

Ojibwe women were very precise about the role of weather in the science of maple sugar cultivation. As they went about their seasonal labor, informants with whom Densmore worked told her, "the best sugar was made when the early part of the winter had been open, allowing the ground to freeze deeper than usual, this being followed by deep snow. They considered the first run of sap as best. Their other observations were that a storm usually followed the first warm weather, and afterwards the sap began to flow again. This sap, however, grained less easily than the first and had a slightly different flavor. Rain produced a change in the taste and a thunderstorm is said to have destroyed the characteristic flavor of the sugar."[31]

Ojibwe women had many uses for maple syrup. It seasoned fruits, vegetables, cereals, and fish and sometimes reduced to thick syrup for compounding with medicines to suit the delicate palates of children. The sugar itself was candy. Densmore wrote, "a woman with a goodly supply of maple sugar in its various forms was regarded as a thrifty woman providing for the wants of her family."[32]

Densmore's ethnography revealed a remarkable tradition of plant and medicinal knowledge hidden within the tiny Indian communities of the Great Lakes. Wild rice and maple sugar were the essential foods. Sweet grass was important for ceremony. Ladyslipper was a toothache remedy, butternut a popular dye. Plant names sometimes had interesting Ojibwe cultural references, such as one taken for rheumatism called Nanabozhoo's grandmother's hair. Ojibwe people used plants and medicines every day for minor bodily complaints like headache or sore throat and occasionally for serious medical conditions. Densmore met Maiingans, an Ojibwe man who related the story of his childhood leg amputations after a severe case of frostbite. His surgeon was an Ojibwe healer who dressed the wounds twice a day with pounded bark. Densmore wrote with admiration, "the healing was perfect."[33] Densmore later observed that working with plants and healing was gender-neutral labor in Ojibwe culture: "All summer the old medicine men and women were gathering and drying herbs so they would have a good supply of medicines and remedies of all sorts."[34]

Densmore's ethnography was highly attentive to the stability of Ojibwe traditions in the early twentieth century and less attuned to the ways in which politics and American colonization were challenging Ojibwe survival in the Great Lakes. Most of her fieldwork came just prior to the emergence of the Jingle Dress Dance, and Densmore never mentioned the practice in her published work or public conversation. On the radio, Densmore introduced Minnesotans to aspects of Dakota and Ojibwe culture they might not otherwise experience. Densmore presented a series about American Indian life in Minnesota on WCCO Radio in Minneapolis during the winter and spring of 1932. A more popular venue for her ethnographic work finally became available during the 1930s, a decade of unprecedented popular interest in American Indian culture in the United States. American Indian artifacts moved into museums by the thousands. It was the decade that John Neihardt interviewed Black Elk in South Dakota and Oliver LaFarge won a Pulitzer Prize for his Indian novel *Laughing Boy*.[35] In the 1930s, anthropologists and intellectuals, as well as politicians in Washington, were distancing themselves from ideas of progress based on race and turning away from long-standing policies of cultural assimilation, exemplified by the allotment of reservations and boarding school education.[36]

It is now a century since Densmore embarked on her important fieldwork among Ojibwe people, but interest in

Native landscapes and the environment, and traditions of indigenous healing has never been greater. Indigenous people throughout North America and the world are remembering their traditional diets, activities, and medicines along with linguistic and cultural revitalizations.[37] The "healing power of music" is no longer a belief confined to American Indians. The Ojibwe Jingle Dress Dance did not disappear, but during the 1980s it made a great leap as it evolved from a regional tradition primarily practiced by small numbers of elderly women to a flourishing, pan-tribal performance with wide appeal across the generations. It has maintained its integrity as a dance of healing. The Red Earth Powwow in Oklahoma now has a category for the Jingle Dress Dance. American Indian traditions of song and dance remain a powerful expression of cultural values. The jingle dress, a gift from the Ojibwe people to a woman of power and vision, has adapted and survived and continues to inspire American Indian women and their communities.

Notes

1. There is remarkably little scholarly literature on the Jingle Dress Dance. Tara Browner's book *Heartbeat of the People: Music and Dance of the Northern Pow-Wow* (Urbana: University of Illinois Press, 2004) discusses the Jingle Dress Dance in some detail, but other recent studies of the powwow only mention it in passing.

2. Many scholars have discussed the controversial Dance Order. See, e.g., Frederick Hoxie, *The Final Promise: The Campaign to Assimilate the Indians* (Lincoln: University of Nebraska Press, 1983), and Lawrence C. Kelly, *The Assault on Assimilation: John Collier and the Origins of Indian Policy Reform* (Albuquerque: University of New Mexico Press, 1983).

3. Commissioner of Indian Affairs Charles Burke issued a government circular, *Indian Dancing,* in 1921.

4. This idea is discussed by ethnomusicologist Thomas Vennum, Jr., in "The Ojibway Begging Dance," in *Music and Context: Essays for John M. Ward,* ed. Anne Dhu Shapiro (Cambridge: Department of Music, Harvard University, 1985), 54–78.

5. Thanks to Marcia Anderson, curator at the Minnesota Historical Society, for showing me jingle dresses in the collection.

6. Patricia C. Albers and Beatrice Medicine, "Some Reflections on Nearly Forty Years on the Northern Plains Powwow Circuit," in *Powwow,* ed. Clyde Ellis, Luke Eric Lassiter, and Gary H. Dunham (Lincoln: University of Nebraska Press, 2005), 26.

7. Browner, *Heartbeat of the People,* 53.

8. Albers and Medicine, "Reflections," 40.

9. "Prayer of healing" is Tara Browner's phrase. Browner also mentions that other tribal groups, the Lakotas and HoChunks in particular, have developed renditions of jingle dress origin stories that incorporate their own tribes in the telling.

10. Brenda Child, *Boarding School Seasons: American Indian Families 1900–1940* (Lincoln: University of Nebraska Press, 1998).

11. National Archives, Record Group 75, Bureau of Indian Affairs, Chicago Branch, Records of the Leech Lake Agency (cited hereafter as NA, RG 75, BIA, CB).

12. Ibid.

13. Ibid.

14. E.g., Katherine Osburn, *Southern Ute Women: Autonomy and Assimilation on the Reservation, 1887–1934* (Albuquerque: University of New Mexico Press, 1998).

15. Barbara A. Babcock and Nancy J. Parezo, *Daughters of the Desert, Women Anthropologists in the Southwest, Biographical Sketches and Selected Bibliographies,* (Tucson: Arizona State Museum, 1986).

16. Densmore's trip to Grand Portage is described in Nancy L. Woolworth, "Miss Densmore Meets the Ojibwe: Frances Densmore's Ethnomusicology Studies among the Grand Portage Ojibwe in 1905," *The Minnesota Archeologist* 38 (August 1979): 106–28.

17. Frances Densmore, "Chippewa Music," *Bureau of American Ethnology Bulletin* 45 (1910); Frances Densmore, "Chippewa Music II," *Bureau of American Ethnology Bulletin* 53 (1913).

18. Foreword to Densmore, "Chippewa Music"; Densmore, "Chippewa Music II."

19. Densmore wrote a biographical sketch of Julia Spears Warren and made this point about the naming of Madeline Island in the Densmore Papers, Collection of the Minnesota Historical Society, St. Paul (cited hereafter as DP). Of course, Ojibwe people had long referred to Madeline Island as Mooniingwanenaning, and it is the heart of the Ojibwe homelands in the Great Lakes.

20. William W. Warren had a short life of twenty-eight years (1825–53). He wrote a classic study published in 1885 by the Minnesota Historical Society as volume 5 of the Collections of the Minnesota Historical Society. The book is still in print as *History of the Ojibway People* (St. Paul: Minnesota Historical Society Press, 1984).

21. Densmore's biographical sketch of Julia Spears Warren, DP. Densmore mentioned the tribal celebration held at White Earth on June 14, 1907. The White Earth Powwow is still held on this date every year. This passage was taken from Densmore's typed introduction of "Prelude to the Study of Indian Music in Minnesota," DP.

22. S. Lieberman, "A Review of the Effectiveness of Cimicifuga Racemosa (Black Cohosh) for the Symptoms of Menopause," *Journal of Women's Health* 5 (1998): 525–29.

23. Frances Densmore, "Uses of Plants by the Chippewa Indians," *Forty-fourth Annual Report of the Bureau of American Ethnology* (Washington, D.C.: Government Printing Office, 1928), 317–18.

24. Ibid., 297.

25. NA, RG 75, BIA, CB.

26. Ibid.

27. Densmore, "Chippewa Music II," 251.

28. Densmore, "Uses of Plants," 322.

29. Frances Densmore, *Chippewa Customs* (St. Paul: Minnesota Historical Society Press, 1979), 128. Densmore's study was first published in 1929 by the Smithsonian Institution, *Bureau of American Ethnology Annual Report, Bulletin 86* (Washington, D.C.).

30. "Making Maple Sugar," in Densmore, "Uses of Plants," 308–13.

31. Ibid., 309.

32. Ibid., 313.

33. Ibid., 332–35.

34. Ibid.; typescript of presentation, WCCO Radio, March 9, 1932, DP.

35. John C. Neihardt, *Black Elk Speaks: Being the Life Story of a Holy Man of the Oglala Sioux* (New York: W. Morrow, 1932); Oliver LaFarge, *Laughing Boy* (Boston: Houghton Mifflin, 1929).

36. For an excellent intellectual history of the assimilation policy, see Hoxie, *Final Promise*. For a history of government boarding schools that emphasizes Ojibwe people, see Child, *Boarding School Seasons*.

37. The World Indigenous Peoples Conferences include presentations on indigenous plants and medicines as part of the program. The meetings attract indigenous peoples from around the globe, including Native Canadians, Native Americans and Hawaiians, aboriginal Australians, the Maori from New Zealand, and other Pacific Islanders.

Contributors

Colin Calloway is Professor of History and the Samson Occom Professor of Native American Studies at Dartmouth College. Professor Calloway has published many books and articles, including *The Scratch of a Pen: 1763 and the Transformation of North America, One Vast Winter Count: The Native American West Before Lewis and Clark* (winner of six "best book" awards), and *First Peoples: A Documentary Survey of American Indian History.*

Brenda Child is Associate Professor of American Studies at the University of Minnesota, where she teaches American Indian history. She has published two books on boarding schools, *Boarding School Seasons: American Indian Familes, 1900–1940,* and, with Margaret Archuleta and K. Tsianina Lomawaima, *So Far Away: Boarding Schools and American*

Indian Families, 1900–1940. Child is an enrolled member of the Red Lake Band of the Chippewa Tribe in northern Minnesota.

R. David Edmunds holds the Watson Professorship of American History at the University of Texas, Dallas, where he teaches Native American history. A prolific historian, Edmunds has authored many publications, including *The New Warriors: Native American Leaders since 1900,* and *Tecumseh and the Quest for Indian Leadership,* (winner of the Alfred Heggoy Prize). He is past president of the American Society for Ethnohistory and the Western History Association.

Laurence M. Hauptman is Distinguished Professor of History at the New Paltz campus of the State University of New York. He is a leading historian specializing in the nineteenth- and twentieth-century northeastern United States. His many books include *The Oneida Indians in the Age of Allotment, 1860–1920, Chief Daniel Bread and the Oneida Nation of Indians of Wisconsin,* and *Conspiracy of Interests: Iroquois Dispossession and the Rise of New York State.* Hauptman has also done a great deal of litigation research and expert witness testimony on behalf of Indian nations.

Albert L. Hurtado holds the Paul H. and Doris Eaton Travis Chair in Modern American History at the University of Oklahoma, where he teaches Native American history. A specialist in California Indians, Hurtado has published many articles and books, including *John Sutter: A Life on the North American Frontier, Indian Survival on the California Frontier,* and, with Peter Iverson, *Major Problems in American Indian History.*

Peter Iverson is Regents Professor of History at Arizona State University. A pioneer of twentieth-century Native American history, his books include *Diné: A History of the Navajos, "For Our Navajo People": Diné Letters, Speeches and Petitions, 1900–1960,* and, with Albert Hurtado, *Major Problems in American Indian History.* He is past president of the Western History Association.

Wilma Mankiller achieved fame as the first woman to become chief of the Cherokee Nation and as a leader of the Indian civil rights movement. She is known as a leading feminist as well as a tribal leader. Mankiller's contributions to her people and to the United States have earned her the Medal of Freedom, the nation's highest civilian award. She is the author of a best-selling autobiography, *Mankiller, a Chief and Her People.*

Index

In this index fictitious persons are shown in quotation marks (e.g., "Red-Bird, Thomas").